SIMPLE TRUTHS
OF EXISTENCE
Book 1

Lighten Up

From Density to Freedom

Channeled and Written by

Greg Campisi

Published by
AWAKEN Center for Human Evolution
a 501(c)(3) Charitable Organization
Quakertown, PA

AwakenCHE.org

Cover design and book layout by Greg Campisi

Written by Gregory Campisi

GregCampisi.com

ISBN: 979-8-9962819-0-9

For my amazing and supportive wife —
Thank you for sharing this crazy,
beautiful journey by my side.

And to our best friend,
and my number one guy,
Jonathan Rosser —
You will always be
remembered and loved
for the bright light you are.

DISCLAIMER

I'm not a fan of disclaimers, but that said, I empathize with humanity's struggles and honor the importance professionals play in our physical and mental health. And so…

The content of this book is intended for informational and inspirational purposes. It reflects the personal experiences, beliefs, and channeled insights of the author and is not intended to diagnose, treat, cure, or prevent any physical, mental, or emotional condition.

This information is not a substitute for professional medical, psychological, or psychiatric care. If you are experiencing mental health challenges, trauma, or any medical condition, please consult a licensed healthcare professional.

Table of Contents

A Note from the Author

This channeled wisdom has become my truth.
I now entrust it to you.

It has changed the way I view everyday life and the interactions I have with others, especially my family. You don't have to believe in spirituality, or even channeling, for this material to shift your own life. I only ask that you open your mind, adopt what resonates, and leave the rest behind.

Allow this book to be a companion on your journey of awakening, guiding you to new perspectives about the truths of our existence. Life often seems challenging, but this material has shown me that it's far simpler than we imagine.

What you're about to read was channeled during a powerful journey of deep meditation and intentional plant medicine. A single question unleashed nearly three hours of profound wisdom, arriving as beautifully simple truth. I knew instantly that this material wasn't just for me — it was brought *through* me to be shared.

I had channeled brief messages before, but nothing like this. This came through on an entirely new level. I didn't push my consciousness aside to let something else speak through me or simply verbalize words I was hearing in my head. I lived it: vivid visions, inner knowing, and powerful energetic experiences flooding my whole being with an intensity I had never known. This book is a translation of those teachings, much like recounting a realistic dream.

After the first channeling, I instinctively knew I had opened a door to a larger universe. The more I surrendered to this process, the more insights continued to flow through me. Each journey brought new revelations. What was meant to be a single book quickly became an entire series of wisdom. I heard the name clearly: *Simple Truths of Existence*.

This material presented itself so simply, honestly, and clearly, it allowed me to easily embrace a new understanding of this existence and the human condition. I wish you could have felt it the way I did. Maybe you will.

Maybe this book will stir something awake, driving you to seek a truth greater than what the world has taught you.

Before we dive in, I'd like to share three core concepts that form the foundation of everything in these pages: *We are here to create and experience creation, creation is a manifestation of energy, and the energy of creation is always in motion.* Every experience, every emotion, every moment we've lived is rooted in these concepts.

As you take in this wisdom, you'll feel what's true for you. Perhaps you won't just read these words — you'll experience them. If it moves you, share it. Use it. Live it.

It is with deep humility and gratitude that I offer you the beginning of our journey together.

Welcome to *Simple Truths of Existence, Book 1.*

Lighten Up: From Density to Freedom

Introduction:
A Glimpse Into My Awakening

This channeling turned my understanding of life around, and I want to share a little about what led to this moment. I hope it helps you understand that our lives are a constant process of unfolding wisdom and uncovering who we truly are.

I've been walking an intentional path of awakening for over twenty years to reach this crossroads. For you, maybe reading this book will instantly spark a shift. Or maybe your awakening will unfold over months, years, or lifetimes. Awakening happens exactly as it should, step by step, truth by truth, when you're ready to accept it.

I've been blessed to receive these profound truths that go far beyond anything my own mind would have conceived. Which raised the question: What opened me to becoming a conduit for this wisdom?

I didn't take a magic channeling pill, but whatever opened, stayed open. Through humility and a willingness to embrace the magic of the unknown, the Simple Truths continue to flow through me.

But before we open a new door, come with me for a moment, back to where it all began…

As a child, I was always drawn to the mystical: ghosts, aliens, psychics, unicorns — you name it, and I loved it. Thinking back, I see how certain moments marked significant shifts in my life, even if I wasn't aware of their impact at the time.

I remember watching the movie *Powder* as a teenager with tears streaming down my face. It wasn't from sadness, but from how powerfully it resonated. Something inside me recognized the potential for humanity that the main character embodied, and I knew that same potential lived within me. I also understood his pain. His isolation. Feeling different and misunderstood. I knew those feelings all too well.

My early years were filled with similar nudges from my spirit like that, much more than I realized. And it was just after turning 30 that I *consciously chose* to embrace my spiritual journey because I met someone who changed my life.

One of my closest high school friends was getting married. I was a groomsman. She was a bridesmaid. I asked her out at the end of the evening — and she turned me down. But the universe had other plans. A few months later, we reconnected at the bride's birthday gathering. This time, something clicked, and we left that night holding hands, eager to see each other again.

As fate would have it, she was a gifted intuitive. The stories she shared with me were fascinating. Her whole family was gifted, especially her mom. I was suddenly plunged into the deep end of spirituality, embracing my new path, or perhaps an expressway, to awakening.

Her mom led gatherings filled with channelings, guided meditations, and even assigned us homework. This included introspective exercises, journaling, and reflection. She offered me access to their library of metaphysical books. As my eyes browsed across over a hundred titles, something in particular stood out: *Conversations with God* by Neale Donald Walsch.

At the time, I was a product designer occasionally traveling to China. My trips were filled with long flights and quiet hotel nights — perfect for reading. I tore through all three books in the series. I remember sitting with Book 1 in my hands, stunned. Life would never be the same. The words in those pages called out to my soul and made sense on every level. I couldn't believe the whole world hadn't read this. Why wasn't humanity already living in peace with such knowledge at our fingertips?

Fast forward about three years. Our relationship unraveled. It was heartbreaking to move on, but a necessary ending to a chapter in both of our books. And as that door closed, another opened.

I realized how important it was to continue along my new spiritual path. I searched for groups and teachers, and in that searching, I saw how many others were on similar journeys. Feeling disconnected from religion. Uncertain about their calling. And alone on their path. That's when I knew. My soul was asking me to create a space for the spiritual community to find support and connection.

I was guided to make it a non-profit, and that's how AWAKEN Center for Human Evolution was born. What began as small groups in my condo quickly grew into something much grander, including expos drawing hundreds of people. It was exciting to continue unfolding alongside others eager to change themselves, and see that change reflected in the world. We were more than a community — we were soul family.

Through a willingness to evolve, I developed a knack for recognizing my faults. But despite all my work and everything we were doing at AWAKEN, I found myself feeling stuck more days than I'd like to admit. Patterns kept resurfacing, telling me there were still parts of myself that I was afraid to see. I would meditate, journal, and get guidance from gifted friends. Don't get me wrong, I had *a lot* of personal revelations, but something bigger needed to shift.

And it did. What came through one amazing evening was my first major channeling and the basis of this book.

As you read these pages, let the words reach a part of you that's been whispering, or maybe screaming, for you to remember the simple truth of life and of who you are. If this book cracks your door open even slightly, it's enough to let the light in. The rest will happen naturally — and maybe we'll shatter some walls and lighten some density in the process.

Now, I invite you to begin our journey together, one that starts in fear and leads to freedom.

Enjoy.

PART 1

The Weight of Being Human

What does it mean to be human? A question we should easily be able to answer, yet possibly one of the most challenging of our lives.

Being human is the most profound experience a soul can choose. It offers moments of deep love and joy, yet bears the weight of unworthiness and the confinements of suffering.

As children, we are joyful and carefree, moving through the world with wonder. As we age, we gather experiences — some vibrant and beautiful, others stressful or traumatic. Life becomes even more complicated as we begin labeling, defending, and suppressing. Eventually, the truth of who we are is buried under layers of beliefs and survival instincts. We continue forward, carrying a heaviness we were never meant to hold onto.

Some of the weight we carry we see clearly, like daily responsibilities and expectations, but we carry much of it unconsciously. Unspoken fears, unprocessed pain, and unreleased emotions are compounding behind the scenes. Mistaking this heaviness for our true identity, we often convince ourselves that healing is beyond our grasp. In reality, most suffering stems from holding onto the past or resisting the present.

To free ourselves from the weight we're bearing, we have to understand how fear and trauma block the natural flow of our life force.

CHAPTER 1:

The Density of Fear

After nearly two decades of meditating, journaling, and peeling back layers through self-reflection, questions still remained. One in particular kept gnawing at me: *Why am I still afraid?*

I wasn't referring to anything like a fear of heights or another world war. This was about the personal and more subtle fears I carried. For instance, despite running AWAKEN for the last twelve years, organizing expos, and pushing myself out of my comfort zone to be a public speaker and host my events, I still held on to a lot of insecurity. Some of these fears had followed me since childhood: *Am I good enough? Will the world accept me for who I am? Do I have to act a certain way to fit in?*

I wondered if I was really helping people, if all the time I put into AWAKEN was worth it, or if it was failing because of me? I also burdened myself with the daily concerns that I wasn't providing for my family or being a good enough parent to my stepchildren. All of these insecurities stemmed from fear, and I could no longer bear their weight.

One quiet evening at home with my wife, we prepared for a deep journey, seeking clarity. Together we created a small altar of crystals, statues, and sacred geometry, then began a short ceremony. We connected to the divine universe above, the sacred Earth below, and called in our spirit team: guides, angels, ancestors, even the ascended masters.

I closed my eyes, focused my intention on receiving guidance, and silently asked: *How do I release fear?*

What I didn't realize on this fateful evening was that by asking this simple question with sincerity and receptivity, a floodgate burst open. I sat in quiet meditation until I felt the energy beckoning me, and my journey began. The wisdom that came through was from somewhere beyond this plane — a higher consciousness that chose to answer in a way that my mind would've never conceived.

The comfort of my home dissolved into a vision, and I found myself immersed in a waking dream.

I was huddled in the corner of a small, dark cave. Saturated with hues of deep purples and blues, the colors reminded me of sadness and depression. Cowering in the corner of this stone enclosure, a chill filled my being. A heaviness overcome me as I shrank into an even tighter knot. I knew immediately that I wasn't merely a bystander to the lessons about to unfold. I was an active participant, viscerally feeling every moment.

A sense of claustrophobia gripped me. I've always been comfortable in small spaces, but this sensation went beyond the tightness of the cold walls of this tiny, dimly lit cave. Something else was closing in on me. My chest tightened, and I began struggling to breathe. I felt a heavy, invisible force pressing in from every direction.

The sensation was so intense, it pulled my physical body to the floor. I instinctively curled into a ball, mirroring the claustrophobic posture of my vision. Rocking back and forth, I was once again a scared child alone in the dark.

This was the energy of fear.

Real learning isn't delivered through answers. It comes through experience. I wasn't merely observing fear. I was inside it, feeling it throughout my being, experiencing it from an entirely new perspective — *energetically*.

I felt my own energy retreating against the force of fear. It was collapsing in, leaving me feeling crushed under a weight that I couldn't see. I was buried. Hidden from the world and even from myself. The sensations overwhelmed me, and I understood how a lack of self-esteem can make us feel invisible and insignificant. As the heavy feelings engulfed me, a word surfaced, capturing the moment perfectly.

Condensed.

The experience was giving me an opportunity to understand fear on a different level. I was inside this cave to realize that the energy of fear was ***dense***.

That single thought sent me tumbling down a rabbit hole where wisdom and science collided. Fear is much more than an emotion or feeling. It's a *specific* kind of energy: a tangible force with unique qualities.

This was the first of many lessons the evening held. When we feel an emotion, we don't just sense it. We embody it fully, taking on its frequency and properties. Fear makes us feel small for a reason: *It energetically condenses us.*

That's when the lightbulb went on. This wasn't just a spiritual insight. It was basic science. Emotions behave energetically, governed by the same physical laws that apply to everything in this universe. So of course our emotions, our own energetic responses to life, follow those same laws.

We often talk about emotions as positive or negative, judging them as good or bad. But this was about understanding, not judging, our feelings. Emotions like fear and anger can be on the negative side of a scale, without them being bad or wrong. They're on that side for a reason: because they're lower vibrational energies, pressing in, condensing us.

Ever notice the tension in your body when you're angry? That's your muscles contracting. When we're in fear, our energy packs so tightly together that we feel smaller, solid, and stuck. Frozen with fear. We become like the walls of that cave: cold, hard, and closed off. The denser the emotion, the heavier we feel.

Positive emotions such as love and joy are the opposite: lighter and higher in vibration. *Less dense*. But we rarely describe something as less dense, so I asked, "What's the opposite of dense?" The answer immediately popped into my awareness: *expansive*.

It was that simple. Negative emotions condense us. Positive emotions expand us.

There it was, a correlation so obvious, all of the physical universe demonstrates it for us. Matter has three states: solid, liquid, and gas. The tighter the particles are packed together, the denser the object is, and the slower it vibrates. The densest objects are solid. Their particles have little freedom to move, like being jam-packed in a small elevator. If those particles could talk, they'd say they feel claustrophobic, like I felt in the cave.

As matter expands, its particles space out. Solid becomes liquid, like ice melting into water, becoming fluid. And as it rises to the next state, it becomes gas, giving its particles even more space. More room to breathe. Gas particles are the most expansive, floating through existence, never feeling stuck or weighed down. If they could speak, they'd say how *free* they feel.

It was such an elegant parallel between our emotional energy and the physical properties of matter. Emotions move and stagnate. They lift us up or weigh us down.

So there I was, curled up on the floor, still rocking back and forth, as the energy of fear pressed in on me like a crushing weight. Not figuratively. *Physically.* I was fully absorbed in its properties. We've all felt the grip of fear, but what we're really feeling when we're afraid is fear's density. Density that clouds our mind, clogs our energy, and burdens our soul.

How have we all come this far without understanding the energetic reality behind our emotions?

And the real kicker? We already talk about emotions in these *exact terms.* We just didn't realize how literal we were being. We've been speaking the language of energy all along.

Something *weighs* on our minds. We feel *heavy-hearted, stuck, under pressure,* or *tied down.* Breakups can feel emotionally *crushing.* When someone is closed to new perspectives, we actually call them *dense.* I was so stubborn as a child, my parents said I was *thick-headed.*

These aren't just metaphors. *They're clues.*

Perhaps the gaze of Medusa reveals more than myth. It talks about being turned to stone. And while fear may not physically turn us to stone, energetically, we solidify.

This experience was going beyond the effect of fear. It was also showing me the consequences of density. That's why my vision placed me in a dark cave. Density blocks light from getting in. It also prevents ours from shining out. It dims our light and severs our connection from everything and everyone. This includes our connection with ourselves and the divine.

When we refer to fear, we're not just talking about panic and terror. Not all forms of fear are obvious. It's a master of disguise, wearing the faces of worry, doubt, insecurity, and countless other masks. A multitude of emotions weigh us down every day, and while we don't always equate them directly to fear, they carry a similar vibration. Energetically, they accumulate, compounding and compressing us more and more in every moment that we feel them. All wrapped around a core: our emotional pain.

While I grappled with these thoughts, the vision changed. Instead of crouching in a dark cave, I now found myself standing in a dimly lit therapist's office. The room was quiet. A person was lying on the couch, eyes closed, digging through layers of memory and pain.

I wasn't just witnessing the session. I was feeling it: the struggles with everyday life, the anxiety, the stress, the grief. I thought about the myriad of people seeking help, spending years in therapy trying to unravel their issues.

My consciousness expanded outward. I could sense the weight of millions feeling the same. They were all struggling to find happiness, searching for the root cause of their pain, looking for the light they lost, and slowly withering in the darkness.

Feeling it all, it became clear: The vibrational density of fear creates an energetic block — a dam in the river of our life force. When we cling to fear, we prevent energy from flowing freely. Without that flow, we cannot heal, evolve, or fully live in the present moment.

As these revelations unfolded, the walls of the office faded. I felt the full weight of our collective fear engulfing me. This was much different from my personal experience inside the cave. This was thicker. Denser. It felt like a weighted blanket smothering the Earth.

Layer upon layer, our collective fear had spread across the planet, compounding over time. It was like a disease that had been growing and strengthening for decades, even centuries. I paused, empathizing for the Earth, for what our energy was doing to her.

As I dove deeper into the collective energy, I sensed other frequencies holding all our fear in place. I began to wonder: *Are we all slaves to something bigger? Are we held in fear by those who wish to control us*?

I couldn't stop the barrage of thoughts that rushed in. Conspiracy theories flooded my mind about technology and media, 5G disrupting our natural frequency, and grander theories about the Illuminati and the Deep State pulling the strings. I began following the thread of collective fear into its dark corners. *Were they purposefully spreading fear and creating frequencies that trap us in this dense energy?*

As my mind spiraled, I felt myself giving in to all the dark possibilities that conspiracies drag us into — but another message and lesson in physics quickly pulled me out. *Denser objects are easier to hold onto and control. Expand your state, and nothing can control you.*

Think of a rock. You can pick it up. Throw it. Break it. Once you put it down, gravity holds it firmly in place. It's the densest state of matter.

Now try to pick up water. It's not so easy. You can cup it into your palms, but it quickly slips through your fingers. You can't break a liquid. It simply parts and reconverges, naturally flowing with its surroundings. You can feel it, even channel it, but its fluidity prevents you from molding it.

Now try to hold air. You can't. There's nothing tangible to grasp. It's too light. Vapor is made of the same particles as ice, but you can't hold a gas, see it, or even feel it — because its particles are too expansive.

Simple Truth: Emotions are energy.
They condense and expand us.

The denser our energy, the easier we're manipulated. It's our density that holds us in place and allows others to grip, shape, and break us. The more expansive we are, the less power over us is possible. Expansion dissolves resistance, and with it, anyone's ability to control us. As we expand into lighter states of being, we don't get stuck on beliefs or caught in the grip of fear. Life passes through us with ease, without collision, without damage.

It's not about trying to stop those who want to control us, because that would mean our freedom depends on changing something outside of ourselves. *Freedom is in our hands, within our own energy.*

I sat there on my floor, feeling it all: my own fear, the collective fear, the conspiracies, and the Earth suffocating beneath it. As tempting as it was to follow the dark thread of collective control, I knew the journey wasn't meant to go there. It's not about controlling the world or the world controlling us. It's about empowering ourselves by freeing our own energy.

It resonated on every level, and with that thought, the energy shifted. I felt myself rising above the weight of the collective fear. The vision changed, shifting to the other side of the spectrum, to the expansive emotions of love and joy.

A warm glow above caught my attention, and I immediately felt the light tingling my skin. I looked up and my eyes were greeted by the brilliant rays of the sun radiating down upon me. In stark contrast to the cave, a lightness permeated my being. I felt my energy lightening up and expanding, as if I was merging with my surroundings.

I looked around and found myself in a meadow, surrounded by flowers. They were all leaning into the sunlight, blooming, expanding their petals, and opening up to life. I was in awe of the sheer beauty of the scene. Time stood still as I allowed myself to just be in this ever-expanding energy.

As I melted into the bliss of the moment, I thought: *Is this what awaits us if we expand past all of our fears?*

More thoughts and questions seeped into my mind, pulling me away from the peaceful energy of the vision. *Why would any of us choose fear over this? Who wants to be cold and alone, condensed in the dark?* Maybe something else was holding us down, keeping us in place — in fear. But it wasn't anything outside of us. That message was clear.

There had to be a missing piece to the puzzle. I felt an urge to return to my original question, so I called out, "How do we release it? How do we release all this fear?"

Instead of the answer coming as a visceral experience, I heard it, simple and clear: *You just release it.*

I laughed. "Oh, sure. Just release it," I called out, refusing to believe something so simple. "We're just supposed to release fear, and we're all good? Like dropping a mic?"

The response came again, gentle and true. *Yes. It's a choice. It's always a conscious choice to release anything.*

Still, my mind resisted. *Could it really be that simple? Are we all suffering needlessly? Do we cry out to God every day for help when the power is in our own hands?*

We have to understand that releasing fear is a conscious effort. It's not like a balloon that slips away if we accidentally loosen our grip. Fear isn't a layer of water that we can shake off like a wet dog. It was a density clinging to us and weighing us down.

With that, I understood why the answer I'd resisted wasn't as simple as it seemed. *We just let go.* Like dropping a ball. If we open our hand, it falls away. So why won't we let go? What's causing us to grip fear so tightly?

Two answers arose.

First, because we won't let go of anything we refuse to recognize. Before we'll release anything, we must first acknowledge we're holding onto it. See it. Own it. And most importantly, admit that we've relinquished our free will to it.

But even when we know our pain intimately, we hold it tightly, as if it's a part of us. We define ourselves by it. So for those of us who know exactly what we're holding on to, we have to go deeper still and ask: *Why are we gripping it so tightly?*

Because many of us believe that fear and suffering aren't just things we carry, but parts of who we are. Permanent. Unavoidable. *Deserved.* As children, we often blame ourselves for how we're treated by others, believing we are bad or deserving of abuse. And if we feel we deserve something, we'll never let it go. When we believe it's ours, part of our being, we continually hold on to it as tight as we can.

I felt myself sinking deeper into the heaviness of fear, asking: *Why would anyone feel they deserve to suffer?*

The answer surfaced as a quiet knowing: Because we feel powerless against circumstances that seem beyond our control. So we adopt the role of *victims*. In doing so, we anchor ourselves deeper into density, gripping fear even tighter. The longer we inhabit the belief we are victims, the more it feels like the truth of who we are. And the more it feels like *our truth*, the harder it becomes to release.

Before we can release fear, we have to release victimhood. The path I was being led down was becoming clearer. A single question had begun this journey, but it could not be fully understood with a single answer. Life compiles on top of itself, interconnected and intertwined. Fear was connected to victimhood, and victimhood was connected to something else, which was connected to something else. I was in for a long night of unraveling the human condition one thread at a time. It was the only way to understand the full tapestry we've woven for ourselves.

Victimhood felt even denser and darker than fear. Those of us who fall into the energy of victimhood, fall in for good reason, but just as it's our choice to release fear, it's also our choice to release victimhood.

And we won't release victimhood until we understand why we are victims. Until we understand that none of us deserve suffering. We have to see that we weren't given the miracle of life only to fill it with pain.

Everything in creation serves a greater purpose, playing its part in the bigger picture that's always unfolding. What I had been shown was only the beginning of this journey.

Something even denser was holding the fear within us, keeping it trapped and pulling us out of the present. This was beyond blocking the flow of our energy, it was crippling it.

Our worries and doubts, our sense of feeling unsafe, even our most intense fears of bodily harm and sexual assault were being trapped in our minds by a powerful force.

My vision shifted again. Beneath the fear, holding it in place and fueling victimhood, something even darker was waiting — *trauma.*

CHAPTER 2:

The Gravity of Trauma

Understanding the energy of fear was only the beginning.

The experience inside the cave showed me fear as a dense emotion. The pressure of fear pushes in, building upon itself, solidifying us. Its density blocks the flow of our energy, like a boulder damming water, but a rock just is. It may stand in the way, but solid matter doesn't actively affect its surroundings.

I felt a new energy emerging. Similar, but different from fear. Stronger. Denser. A darkness consumed my vision, and a relentless energy began pulling from within the shadows. It was so dense, it didn't just block the flow of energy — *it reversed it.*

Beneath the weight of fear was *trauma.*

If fear is the weight we hold onto, trauma is the force that holds onto us. As I felt into this new energy, the darkness that had overtaken my vision coalesced into a single, black spot. I felt its raw power pulling me towards it, and a knowing flooded my being. I instantly understood.

To fully grasp the density of trauma, I was witnessing one of the densest phenomena in the known universe.

A black hole.

Once again, the language of physics was the key to understanding our own energy. A black hole is a massive amount of matter compressed into an unimaginably dense point. It collapses under its own weight, creating an immense gravitational field. Its gravity is so strong that *not even light can escape it.*

The crushing weight of fear I had felt now paled in comparison to the force of trauma. The pull was unfathomable. While fear builds layers around us, blocking our light, trauma pulls from within. Our trauma feels dark for a reason, as if it's draining our life away. Energetically, it is.

Each trauma we endure creates a black hole within our field. Its fierce pull consumes our life force, absorbing our inner light. This is *the energy of trauma.*

Trauma isn't just a wound or a memory. It cuts far deeper than that. It strikes at the core of who we are, making us feel powerless, helpless, and even worthless. Fear and victimhood surround it, mask it, and fuel it — but trauma is the gravity beneath it all, pulling us away from the present and dragging our thoughts and energy into the past.

Fear presses in from all around us, including the media, the government, and often from our own friends and families. But when faced with this external fearful pressure, we have a choice to accept or reject it. Trauma is different. It lives inside us, hauling our energy toward the darkness within. Devouring us. Collapsing our light. Draining our life force.

But there's more. Because we're emotionally tied to the incident that caused our trauma, it becomes something else. The black hole of trauma becomes a wormhole: A bridge through time and space. Our trauma tethers us to a moment that has long since passed. Each time we think about the trauma, or something reminds us of it, we're pulled back in time, reliving it as though it's happening right now. The past becomes the present, and the present gets pulled into the past.

The vision changed, and I found myself standing on a beach. The sound of waves ebbing and flowing filled the air as my toes sifted through the sand. I looked out across the vast ocean, noticing something rising in the distance. A tidal wave was building, growing bigger with each passing moment. As I watched this immense wall of water race toward me, I wasn't afraid. I was in awe, knowing its purpose.

This enormous wave was our life force energy, a force of nature far more powerful than we've ever been taught to believe. Each of us carries that magnitude within us — a tidal wave of creation. That wave is always moving forward through time, because that is the only direction life moves. Watching it approach, I was humbled by the power we all hold.

As the massive wave drew closer, something shifted within it. In the center of the wave, the water spiraled into a massive whirlpool. As the vortex pulled water backwards into its core, the wave began collapsing into itself. This was the wormhole of trauma. The force of creation moves forward while trauma creates a tear in the present, pulling our energy back to the moment of wounding.

The wave slowed almost to a halt, as the force of the vortex fought against the forward momentum of the wave. The unstoppable current of creation battling the immovable gravity of trauma. Neither winning.

This is what trauma does, what it feels like to be caught between the life we want and the past we haven't released. Life is trying to move forward, and something inside us is pulling it back, drawing us back into the dense moment of our pain.

As our energy gets pulled backward, it feeds on the fear of the original wound, growing denser, tearing at the present with increasing force.

When fear is pressing down from the outside and trauma is pulling from within, they combine forces. Their compounded energy, going against the natural flow of creation, makes it almost impossible to stay fully aware in our present life. That unnatural flow of energy affects everything, including our mental clarity, our connection with ourselves, others, nature, and the divine.

I understood why so many of us feel trapped. Beyond stuck — trapped. Caught in a gravity we can't see, leaving us drained and weakened. It's no surprise so many of us feel like we're not fully here. Because we're not. We're emotionally and mentally bound to the energy of our trauma.

This is why our lives become consumed with fear and victimhood. They intertwine with trauma, becoming inseparable, feeding on each other in a vicious cycle. Whether we're a victim of random chance or intentional abuse, we hold onto a fear that it can happen again. And for those of us who feel the trauma was deserved, on some level we *expect* it to keep happening. We become afraid of reliving the past and terrified it will happen again at any moment. As all the density compounds, it reinforces the gravity of trauma, creating a powerful, magnetic vortex pulling us even deeper into the darkness.

Each time we're triggered, fear rushes in, adding another layer of density. Our light collapses inward, like a dying star slowly consuming itself.

Simple Truth: Trauma is so dense, its gravity reverses the flow of life.

For an experience to fracture us this deeply, it has to strike at the core of our being. And while trauma may come from extreme experiences such as violence, abuse, or sexual violation, it doesn't always show itself so obviously. Trauma lives on a vast spectrum, arising from seemingly smaller wounds, like being shamed or yelled at as a child. Regardless of scale, it tears at our soul, reverses the flow of our creative life force, and diminishes the truth of who we really are. It prevents us from speaking, acting, and living authentically.

With each traumatic experience, we develop more trauma points, losing more of ourselves. We're sucked into the gravitational pull of their darkness, feeling incomplete. The dense energy of trauma drags us away from the only thing that truly matters — the present. Depleted and drained of vitality, we are left at our breaking point. We long to surrender to the weight of pain and fear, having lost the energy to overcome them.

How can true freedom exist while fear and trauma rule our energy field? Even if it's hard for us to name, a feeling is always there, a gnawing sense that we're not quite whole, that some part of us is missing.

Eventually the gravity of our trauma grows so strong, it doesn't just drain our own life force, it starts affecting others. When this happens, we become energy vampires, pulling in the energy of anyone who gets too close.

The more trauma points we carry, the stronger our gravitational field, and the more drama surrounds our lives. It becomes an outward cry for help. Our trapped energy screams to be freed. In an attempt to fill the void, we pull others into our drama, subconsciously hoping someone else can either bear what we can no longer carry or free us from it entirely. We feel incapable of creating the life we want, and unintentionally draw from the energy of others.

And we've all felt it from the other side, too. We've been around people whose density pulls at us, demanding our energy to fill an emptiness that nothing outside of them can ever fill. Their pain is so dense and unresolved that simply being near them is exhausting, and our natural reaction is to pull away or demonize them. Hence the label: energy vampire.

Yet the darkness of a black hole doesn't make it evil. It's just matter compressed beyond its natural limits. The same is true for us. As energy vampires, we're compressed by our own unhealed pain, adversely affecting those around us. We're not intentionally draining others. We've forgotten who we are.

Most of us aren't even aware we're doing it. But others feel it. They hear it. They see it. They feel us pulling them in, draining their energy. But rather than judge ourselves as vampires, when we understand trauma energetically, it allows us to hold more empathy and compassion for ourselves and others.

Our trauma doesn't need to be judged. It needs to be freed. When you feel that pull, that irritation, that inexplicable reaction to someone else's trauma or drama — it's a signal. Not about them. About you. It means there is unhealed trauma within you, too. We call that signal a *trigger.* And our triggers reveal exactly where our own energy is stuck.

This was the next lesson.

PART 2

The Misconception of Protection

When the weight of life becomes overwhelming, our survival instincts take over: fight or flight. We suppress or defend, often both. Somewhere along the way, we adopted the belief that protection means avoidance and ignorance. We learned to disregard what is — our own emotional pain. If we hide our pain, ignore our triggers, and avoid discomfort, we think we'll stay safe. But the truth is, these defenses become the walls of our own prison.

Protection was never meant to be a way of life. It was a momentary response, not a permanent state. Yet many of us have built identities around avoidance, mistaking numbness for peace and disconnection for strength.

We tend to view protecting ourselves as righteous and protecting others as heroic. What we rarely admit is that *protection comes from fear.*

True protection isn't about letting fear prevent life from happening. It's about embracing fear through awareness. Most of us weren't taught this. We inherited a model from society, and typically from our parents, where protection is often fear wearing a noble mask.

What we have yet to realize is that the more we try to protect ourselves and others, the more we resist our own healing. We deflect our pain, hide our trauma, and wall in our unprocessed emotions.

CHAPTER 3:

The Gift of Our Triggers

So there I was, still feeling the density of fear and the gravity of trauma, and the night was far from over. More lessons were waiting.

A question kept echoing in my mind: *If we can choose to release fear, can we also choose to release our trauma?*

The answer was swift: *We can, but we don't allow ourselves to.*

Many of our traumas are unhealed because when they are subtle, we don't believe we have any, and when they're more intense, we can't emotionally handle the thought of them. Either way, they remain hidden and unresolved. That dense energy creates a frequency we get trapped in, amplified by fear and constricting the flow of our life force.

I don't know if I intuitively felt into what was next, or if it felt into me. The next piece was apparent. When we refuse to see something in ourselves, the universe finds ways to point it out—through our *triggers*.

During my decades of inner work, I've gotten better at acknowledging my triggers. Better, but still not perfect. It usually goes like this: I ignore them, my wife points them out, I deny them, then silently mutter, "Crap, now I have to look at this."

All jokes aside, it was time for me to face the density. I called out into the vastness of wisdom for more guidance. "Help me understand the triggers." I repeated it again and again, with intention, and the lessons continued.

A new visual filled my mind's eye. This time, I was seeing a parent and child having an interaction. The child was being himself, acting like a kid, while the parent began filling with frustration. I could see and feel the energy of the adult quickly shift from agitation into outright anger. Much to my surprise, the child didn't react. Instead, he calmly walked up to his father, and began physically poking him, edging his dad to the brink of explosion. The dad swatted the little hand away, yelling, "Don't touch!"

Seeing this interaction, I understood what was happening beneath the surface. The black hole that trauma leaves in our energy field becomes sensitive. That trauma point is a tender, energetic wound: swollen, hurting, and not yet healed. Triggers are defensive reactions to these sore spots being poked, signaling where density interrupts our flow.

I was witnessing something many of us have lived through, myself included — a parent being triggered by their child. As the adult's trauma point was being nudged in my vision, I felt into the reaction so strongly that I couldn't contain myself. I shouted out, "Don't touch! Don't touch my tender energy!"

It's easy to blame our emotional outbursts on a child, but the reaction was never about them. It's always about the energy underneath. About our wounds. Our trauma. We're triggered because of our own unhealed pain, not because of what someone else does or says.

The child was quite literally pointing out where the adult's trauma point was, where the energy was stuck, where it needed to be freed. Ideally, I imagine the parent would thank the child and do what was necessary to heal, to get their energy flowing again. But instead, it's an opposite reaction.

Even if we haven't had this interaction with our own child, we've all seen it. We're at a store witnessing that exact moment when an adult is triggered, reacts, and explodes in emotion. And if you're like me, you watch, feeling for the child, wishing to stop the interaction, and thinking, *I'll never treat my child that way* — until we do.

That's precisely what triggers are: life pressing down on our tender spots, reminding us of the pain we haven't healed. They show us precisely where we're hurt. Where our energy needs to be freed.

Triggers are the key to unlocking our blocked energy. We all have them, yet most of us ignore them or become angry at others for seeing them. Regardless of how subtle or deeply buried our traumas are, our triggers have an unmistakable way of revealing them. If physical pain signals where our bodies need healing, triggers signal where our emotions need healing. Where the energy needs releasing.

Think about physical pain for a moment. We view it as something bad because of how it feels. But pain is actually an alert system. It's telling us that something is out of alignment and needs restoration. When something hits us hard enough, the body bruises and swells. While it's healing, the area is sensitive and tender. Hit the same area, and it sends significant pain shooting through the body, sometimes hurting even more than the initial impact. The same is true for our emotional wounds.

The slightest reminder of our trauma sends shockwaves through our whole system. It's like a fresh wound being hit.

The psyche armors itself. We recoil. Our defenses rise. Our survival instincts kick in. And once we know a bruise hurts to be touched, we stop allowing anything near it, preemptively defending it out of fear of feeling that pain again.

We shield and bury trauma rather than expose and heal our emotional wounds. But it only grows more sensitive. The deeper we bury it, the more it festers. The tighter we guard it, the louder our triggers become.

But there's one glaring difference between our physical wounds and our emotional wounds. The body knows how to heal itself. We don't. We're not taught how to heal emotionally. And yet, if we would lighten our grip around trauma and fully feel and free it, we'd instantly shift our lives. And that is one of the easiest and hardest things we'll ever have to do.

Ironically, when other people are triggered, we see it clearly. We see where they're holding onto pain, where they need to let go, and where they need to expand their energy and lighten up. But our own triggers? We refuse to acknowledge them, clutching our own density with everything we have.

And here's another twist. The pain we protect is the very pathway to our freedom. It's where our life force needs our attention, crying out to be freed. We allow the fear of feeling our pain to outweigh the promise of lasting relief.

Until we find our way to healing, our emotional wounds stay tender, reactive, and sensitive to the slightest touch. If we stay afraid of our own pain, we'll never let it go. The longer we hold onto our density, the longer it holds us captive.

Like rulers guarding treasure behind walls, moats, and gates, we fortify our trauma, hiding it deep within our inner castle. Our triggers are the guards, sounding the alarm the moment anyone approaches. And our clever minds find a multitude of subtle, and not so subtle, ways to divert attention from those tender places.

By protecting the wound, we only seal it in. We trap ourselves in the very prison we built to keep ourselves safe. We were never meant to be prisoners to our pain.

One of the most powerful ways life points us toward healing is through the people around us. We can react just as harshly to a stranger's comment as we do to our partner's tone, but typically the ones who poke us the hardest are our family. Kids have an uncanny knowing of where their parents are accumulating the most density. They can feel the stuck energy and go straight to it. And how do we respond? We react through our triggers with anger, guilt, and frustration, shaming and punishing our children for trying to help free our energy.

When anything or anyone reminds us of our pain, we instinctively react. We miss the message entirely. Our loved ones aren't here to drive us crazy; they're here to help us heal. We're all here to release our pain — not suppress it.

As uncomfortable as our triggers feel, they are helpers, not enemies. Our wounds reveal themselves one way or another, crying out and alerting the world that we're suffocating under the weight of fear and being pulled into the gravity of our trauma.

Throughout the night, I had been narrating my visions and messages to my wife, doing my best to translate the experience. As the insights continued to flow, I clearly understood how triggers were the compass pointing directly to the stuck energy longing to be freed. Acting it out, I pointed to a spot in the air and said to my wife, "This is the spot where the energy needs to release..."

BOOM!

At the exact moment that I said *release*, a neighbor set off fireworks. The explosion rattled the house, startling us both. We literally heard and felt an explosion — a release of energy.

My wife and I burst out laughing at how strongly the universe had made its point. It's comical how often we miss blatant signs illuminating our path, but this message was impossible to miss.

Simple Truth: We're triggered to point out where the energy is stuck and needs to be released.

Triggers are the voice of our trapped energy, begging to be set free so we can live fully in the flow of life. They are, in the truest sense, a gift to ourselves.

And while our triggers may point the way, we're the ones keeping ourselves imprisoned. It's up to us to restore the flow, but I was about to learn there was something else blocking our way to freedom.

CHAPTER 4:

The Barriers We Build

We are caught in a seemingly infinite, generational cycle of being traumatized and traumatizing others. The wisdom leading me along this path wasn't just showing me our emotional reactions and actions. It wanted me to understand it all on a deeper level.

Earlier, I had witnessed a father being triggered by his son. The child in the vision was calm, but what really happens to a child when their triggered parent explodes? This is where fear and trauma are born. And for me to fully experience it, things were about to be turned upside-down.

The neighbor's fireworks had snapped me out of my tender energy monologue, but I swiftly sank back into my vision.

I was seeing my father standing in front of me, but we weren't eye to eye. Looking up at him, I quickly realized that I was much smaller. Now I was the young child triggering *my* dad, and in turn, the one being scolded. He was yelling at me for something I did, and I was beyond terrified by his reaction. I stood there silent, holding back my tears.

My father wasn't cruel in any way. Quite the opposite. He was an amazingly loving and cheerful man. If he had a white beard, people would mistake his rosy smile for that of Santa Claus. That's why in the rare times he exploded, it was traumatizing for me. To witness someone always smiling, laughing, and joking suddenly flip and burst into anger — that's all it takes to create a trauma point.

What I did to trigger him wasn't shown to me. Only the energy of the moment mattered. I was brought into this scene to feel myself at the moment of a trauma. I stood there as an innocent child, one moment enjoying the world, and the next, buried under a landslide of dense emotion.

The emotions were overwhelming, and a story my father had shared with me about his father came to mind. I never met my grandfather because he passed away before I was born, but I've seen photos. He was quite literally a stereotypical Italian from Brooklyn, wearing a white tank top, with a pipe hanging out of his mouth.

My dad once described the moment he told his father that he was joining the air force. My father was leaving home, leaving the family business, and leaving his family behind. My grandfather was so enraged, he began yelling, screaming, and cursing at my dad. In a dramatic show of how betrayed he felt, he ripped his shirt open, sending buttons flying across the room. Because my father knew how angry his father would be, he enlisted first, and told him second. That's how much anger my grandfather held onto, and how much unhealed pain he carried.

As I processed these raw feelings, I witnessed the cycle: My father still carried unhealed anger from his father, which was passed to me. Even in my innocence, I triggered him. He reacted. I became traumatized by his anger and carried that into my adulthood and parenthood. I would then be triggered by my stepkids, yell at them, and perpetuate the cycle of passing down unhealed emotions.

In that moment, there was more happening than I realized. As I was scolded, I felt my childhood energy shift on an unconscious level, away from my innocence and joy. I burst out, "There it is!"

Throughout our lives, our personal frequency shifts in relation to the energies around us. As children, when our energy is open and loving, we welcome all energy into our being. As we get traumatized and filled with fear, our energy densifies, restricting our experience of life.

As I felt the energy of anger piercing me, I couldn't handle it. I felt myself shutting down. What had I done to invoke this reaction from my loving father? *Was I a bad child? Was I the cause of this barrage of emotion?* I felt myself collapsing under its weight. I never again wanted to be the target of someone else's anger or experience how it made me feel.

And there it was.

I felt it happen in real time — the moment a child decides the world is no longer safe. The moment the first brick in the wall is placed. I made an unconscious choice out of fear and survival that would affect me for the rest of my life.

What none of us realize is that when we're afraid, threatened, or hit with an emotional energy we can't handle, a survival mechanism kicks in. Our energy hardens, and we create a protective barrier to block out that emotional energy from penetrating us again.

It then becomes our responsibility, as adults, to make a conscious choice to counter it. That's why you and I are both here, to become more aware of the unconscious energy we've created, and consciously change it. We'll get to that soon enough.

But before I go further, I want to pause and honor my father.

I am humbled and blessed by the life my parents provided. Trauma comes in many forms and on many levels. Those of us who grew up without severe abuse, like me, were still affected on some level, such as being yelled at by a parent. My father was in no way mean or abusive. He was full of joy, understanding, and love. He also wasn't perfect because he wasn't fully healed. Even the best parents carry their own trapped emotional blocks and density. As his child, it was very much my job to press his tender spots and trigger him.

You're welcome, dad!

I jest, but triggering our parents comes with consequences. If we were traumatized by the powerful vibration of anger as a child, we're often left believing we caused it. That we created someone else's pain. That we must have deserved what followed—along with all the trauma that accompanied it.

This misconception brings on blame, shame, guilt, and a cascade of dense emotions that *dam* the flow of our life force and *damn* ourselves in the process. There's no coincidence in that double meaning. That's how clever, and obvious, life is.

Each time we're hit energetically, we reactively strengthen our wall, adding more density, blocking out the unwanted vibration, and perpetuating a cycle as old as humanity itself. We build these walls by altering the natural state of our energy, contracting, slowing, and tightening it into density. The more we try to protect ourselves, the denser our energy becomes.

In our innocence and ignorance, believing these walls protect us, we don't realize the consequences of our actions. The denser the wall, the less freely our life force flows. And two other things happen simultaneously: We block unwanted energy outside of ourselves, and also suppress and trap it within. What we keep out, we also keep in.

In creating this energetic shield, we also create a belief that something is bad. In doing so, we decide it doesn't belong —that we should never feel it again.

Just imagine if you decided to block out a color of the rainbow. You didn't like the way red felt, and so you eliminated it from reality. We're not here to *undo* creation, we're here to experience it, and create *more* of what we want.

Our aversion to anger sends a signal to our psyche that anger isn't safe. We then become triggered by angry people, volatile situations, and reminders of our original trauma. In suppressing any emotion, we also limit our energy flow. And the very energy we're trying to keep out is now pressing against our door, trying to get in.

But the energy doesn't want in so that it can stay. *It wants through.*

This was the next lesson. After experiencing each part of life, we're meant to continue on. Our job is to allow the energy of creation to pass through, not try to prevent it, trap it, or hold onto it.

Simple Truth: Energy doesn't just want in, it wants through.

The energy knocking on our door wants to be acknowledged, felt, and released. It wants us to experience it so we can peacefully say: *Yes, I'll take more of that,* or *no thank you, you may go.* But instead of allowing it to pass through, we build a denser wall to keep it out.

Just as the expansiveness and lightness of a gas allows all things to pass through, we are meant to do the same. Solidifying our energy into dense walls prevents life from flowing. Causes conflicts. Clashes. Wars. We're meant to lighten up our energy, rising to a higher state, and allowing all things to pass through.

We're all born in that open state of energy, but density collapses our true, joyous, loving self. Energy is meant to flow freely, and when we harden, blocking its flow, it stalls. It stagnates. Pressure builds, heading for an eruption, or worse.

The body was designed to flow, and when the flow stops, the body reflects that blockage in the only language it has: illness, pain, disease, and breakdown.

Stress can cause heart attacks. Arteries build up plaque and narrow. Blood thickens. Vessels lose elasticity. All of these restrict the flow of blood to the heart as the body becomes more dense. And what causes strokes? Clots. Another form of density.

Think about the solid stone walls of the cave. Impenetrable. Nothing passes through, not even light. When we solidify, we become so dense that light can't get in — and our own light can't shine out. What happens to us emotionally when we shut out the light of the world and seal our own light in?

Depression.

One of our densest emotions, often caused by the pressure we put on ourselves and not living up to the pressure and expectations of others. And what's the leading cause of suicide? Depression. We're affected by so much pressure every day. Deep pressure. Depression. It's right there in the word.

Our density is quite literally *killing us.*

But life is always pointing the way towards healing, attracting experiences that trigger us, and offering a pathway to freedom. Yet instead of seeing those triggers as the invitation for freedom that they are, we often do the opposite — reinforcing the walls, building them higher, thicker, denser.

What else does extreme pressure create? The hardest known substance on Earth: a diamond. We celebrate it as a symbol of love, perhaps because it's unbreakable, but energetically, a diamond is the ultimate wall. Impenetrable. And yet before the pressure, it was carbon, the same material found in the soft graphite point of a pencil. We were hardened by density and pressure, and we're the only ones who can uncompress ourselves and return to a state of expansion.

So here we are, humanity, still believing we have to protect our traumas rather than release them. Still building walls. The timeless tale of *The Three Little Pigs* suddenly holds new meaning.

Each little piggy built their house from different materials: straw, sticks, and bricks. Which house withstood the Big Bad Wolf? Brick. Why? The densest material also offered the most protection.

Energetically, we do the same thing. But instead of brick walls, we build vibrational barriers. When people are emotionally cut off, we say they're hiding behind their walls. We already knew we were doing it. We just didn't understand how literal it was. Emotions are a form of energy, and the walls we build are very real.

So who's afraid of the Big Bad Wolf? We are. The moment we feel threatened and let fear take over, we react, fortifying our homes. We shift our vibrational frequency, condense and harden our energy, and build the densest wall we can muster — all to withstand the wolf at our door who we believe has come to devour us.

But we were never meant to live behind walls of fear. We were meant to live in flow. We're not here to be afraid of the wolf. We're here to understand it. It's at our door hungry for healing, howling in unresolved pain.

But there's a twist: In many cases, that wolf at our door is our own family. It often feels like they're devouring our innocence, but it's only because they lost theirs and were never taught how to reclaim it.

Even in the happiest of homes, our issues, trauma, and density get passed on, generation after generation. The cycle continues until someone brings enough awareness to finally stop it. That's the hope of this book.

If we'd been taught as children how to handle emotions, we wouldn't be so easily traumatized. If we understand that other people's triggered reactions belong to them, not us, we wouldn't be so quick to take on the weight of someone else's unhealed pain. But we weren't taught, and because we so often learn from example, we learn the opposite of healing: hide, protect, deflect. As sensitive, empathic children, we absorbed what was modeled around us, and we mistook it for truth.

We've inherited our parents' walls, built our own, and reinforced all of them, constricting more and more of our life force every time. But that isn't the only consequence of our walls.

CHAPTER 5:

The Deflection of Energy

I was always fascinated by science, and there's one lesson that has stuck with me to this day: For every action, there's an equal and opposite reaction. The consequences of our walls were about to reveal why we traumatize each other, often unintentionally. Throughout the evening, one message stood out above all else — *energy has to move.*

Creation has no agenda except to keep creating. And to do that, the energy of creation has to keep flowing. When we create a block or hold onto a trauma, we stop creative life force from moving through us. That energy doesn't just disappear. It keeps pounding against our walls, trying to get through.

As adults with our vibrational barriers up, we believe we're protecting ourselves. We've shifted our energy to lock out unwanted vibrations, emotions, and experiences that reflect our trauma. We hold onto a false sense of security, believing our walls can prevent us from ever feeling those same traumatizing frequencies again.

We talk about walls and density, but our barriers aren't actually made of stone. We're not talking about an army invading our castle. Our walls are energetic, which creates a very different response to threats.

A new revelation entered my awareness. When we feel threatened by life and by dense energies trying to get through, we create a shift in our vibration to fortify our field and keep them out. But when the dense energy we're keeping out hits our barrier, life doesn't just turn the other cheek. Something else happens.

It reverberates.

It keeps pounding at our door until it finds a new path, and we're the ones who inevitably choose which direction that is.

Imagine walking along and unexpectedly bumping into an invisible barrier. You're deflected back, confused. So you push harder. Again and again, trying to get by. Trying to pass through. Maybe you run and throw yourself against it with all your might, hoping to break it down.

But the barrier doesn't budge. It only pushes back. And so do you, over and over again. You want to keep moving in your current direction, not go back from where you came. There's no easy way around, so you keep banging against that wall, hoping it will let you through, or hoping to weaken and eventually break it. Energy is the same way. It keeps moving forward, not back.

This is how our energetic walls behave. The harder we try to keep energy out, the more it presses back against us. When we don't let it through, it doesn't go back from where it came. It doesn't vanish. The pressure builds, like someone pounding on a door we refuse to open. It keeps knocking harder and harder until we either take down our barrier — or explode from the insanity of life's persistence.

The energy keeps repeating, *let me through*. But our wounded ego, overflowing from holding too much past energy, misinterprets it as: *Let me in. I'm here to hurt you again.*

And we think, *Why me? Why does this keep showing up in my life?* Or we may even think, *Of course trauma is at my door again. This is what I deserve.* And then we scream out, "Why is the universe punishing me?"

The truth is, the universe is really saying: *I love you, and I am here to remind you of what you forgot to let go of.*

It's whispering to us: *Let down your wall. Open yourself up. I only wish to pass through so I can continue my journey of creation, and you can continue yours.*

Creation wants to continue with new creation, and we're standing in its way. We're either trying to block it or trying to send it back, believing parts of creation aren't meant to exist. But we can't send creation back. We can't uncreate life. It's meant to keep moving, to keep creating. The only way to live in flow with life is to allow it, experience it, and continue on.

This visceral feeling of energy being blocked and reverberating against my field was channeling through me. I felt the energy moving through my hands. I intuitively started clapping them, swiftly but softly, mimicking the reverberation of energy against our walls.

Clap. Clap. Clap. Then louder. *CLAP! CLAP! CLAP!* Faster. *CLAP CLAP CLAP CLAP CLAP!* Until my hands were red and pulsating, forcing me to stop.

The message was clear: When we block something, the energy remains. And it doesn't dissipate — *it amplifies.* And we keep experiencing more and more of it, driving us mad, until we let it through.

I stood there, feeling the energy reverberating against my field, over and over again. The energy was impossible to resist. *Clap clap clap clap clap* went my hands again.

I felt it even stronger. Reverberating. Trying to get through. I needed to translate the full intensity of the energy and began pounding on the counter.

Bang! Bang! Bang!

Building momentum and force.

BANG! BANG! BANG! BANG!

Over and over.

BANG! BANG! BANG! BANG! BANG!

Until my hands ached, and I physically couldn't take the sting anymore. I stopped, staring down at my red, throbbing hands, thinking, *Why would I hurt myself just to get a point across?* The message was literally beaten into me: *Blocking energy only leads to more pain, and eventually, madness.*

So the very barrier we build to protect ourselves from anger, for example, intensifies the thing we're trying to avoid. In our ego's hope to prevent more pain, we increase our experience of it, because it keeps pounding against our door.

And while energy pounds against our walls from the outside trying to get through, something equally powerful is happening within. The anger, fear, and pain that we locked inside, the energies we repressed, are fighting just as hard to get out. Like a caged wild animal, it howls. It claws. It searches for any way to get out: to move, to release, to be free.

Suppressed energy always finds ways to move. In trying to protect ourselves, we created a ticking time bomb. We try to ignore it, but it's still there, reverberating against our walls, calling out to be heard, acknowledged, and felt.

If we only would have allowed anger to pass through, we could've moved on. By holding up a stop sign, we keep it with us. It sits at our door, waiting for the green light to move on, declaring: *I am part of life, part of creation. I cannot be ignored. I cannot be uncreated, only transformed.*

The more afraid we are to let something pass through us, the louder it gets, the stronger it grows, and the more afraid we are to face it. Maddened by its incessant persistence, we're left with only one choice: to send it away.

So we deflect it.

We have to relieve the madness, and we scream out, "I can't take this energy any more, you take it!"

Hoping for a moment of relief, we inevitably pass it on, redirecting it to the people closest to us.

This is why we project our emotions. Why we pass on our traumas. And yet, it's not personal and rarely even intentional. It's simply energy following the path it's given as it makes its way through life.

I know that to anyone who has experienced deep trauma, this may seem overly simplified, but I promise you, all of our experiences are expressions of energy — some joyous, some horrific.

This is why many of us unintentionally wound our children. When we won't release our own trauma or heal what caused it, we end up passing that anger onto those we have control over. *Our kids.*

This is why adults who abuse others were likely abused themselves.

The energy is too strong to stop, and so we often act it out, recreating the same trauma in another. When we trap the energy of abuse within us, it becomes us. And because we didn't heal it, we became the abuser. If we don't accept and release the energy of anger, we become angry.

Simple Truth: What we don't heal, we pass on to others.

In our everyday lives, we're constantly triggered and react to the world and the people around us. Blocked energy and emotions build pressure within us, culminating in two outlets, often happening simultaneously. It turns inward, manifesting as physical disease, anxiety, or mental illness. Or it flows outward onto others in various subtle and not-so-subtle forms.

When subtle, it's like a pressure valve: passive aggression, sarcasm, and cutting remarks offering momentary release but no lasting relief. When it erupts, it becomes a volcano of tantrums, outbursts, and physical abuse, spewing unresolved pain onto everyone around us.

Some of us genuinely try to hold it in, believing that containing our pain protects the people we love. But even with the best intentions, unhealed energy always finds a way out. It seeps into our tone, our reactions, our silences. No matter how hard we try, we can't spare others from the energy of what we haven't released within ourselves.

It's not a personal attack, even though it often feels that way. This is energy moving, rejected and redirected, instead of processed and released. That unhealed energy ripples into our relationships, creating an endless cycle of pain causing pain, trauma creating trauma.

I call it: *passing on the pain*.

The wounds we carry from deep fear, abuse, or terror create massive blocks that can take years, even lifetimes, to unravel. But we also pass on our pain in less obvious ways.

When we encounter situations that irritate, frustrate, or offend us, we deflect that accumulated energy outward, often unconsciously, onto whoever is nearby. We ease the pressure of our trauma by releasing it as *drama.*

We've become so ingrained in our pain, so attuned to our drama, that it pervades not only our lives but our entire culture. We built an entertainment industry around it. We tune in nightly to watch strangers argue, struggle, and break down — because somewhere in their chaos, we feel a little less alone in ours.

If a vase has a crack in it, the water doesn't burst out. It leaks out. We're the same. When we believe we're broken, we'll often try to ignore our fears, pains, and trauma, but they still leak out into the world, affecting those around us. We have so many channels that leak unprocessed issues into the world. Some appear so consistently as part of how we communicate, we don't even notice it.

One in particular creates barriers to entire ideas, groups of people, and ways of being. Dare I say it — the word hit me like a brick wall. *Judgement.*

CHAPTER 6:

The Walls of Resistance

I let out a long sigh as I felt deeper into our barriers and all the ways we prevent the flow of life. The lessons weren't slowing down, and something new was surfacing.

It wasn't an extreme energy such as blocking out traumatic emotions. This was something much subtler emerging that creates barriers to life and adds layers of density to our energy. It's something we do unconsciously that prevents us from experiencing the world unfolding around us. Something we do every day without realizing the deeper effect it has on us, others, and creation — *judgement.*

We judge ideas, beliefs, habits, styles. It's so profoundly embedded in our lives, the list is practically endless. If it's part of reality, then someone, somewhere has judged it. We often judge things we dislike as bad, or altogether wrong. Some even take it to the extreme, believing that all of life would be better off if these things were erased from the world.

I began feeling the energy of judgement surrounding me. Surrounding all humanity. It carried its own density, but was unique compared to the other energies I had experienced this evening. It wasn't a pushing or pulling force. Instead, it was more of a tightening, constricting my breathing. I took in a long, slow breath, forcing air inside my lungs, like trying to breathe thin air on a mountaintop. I could barely get enough oxygen. The energy of judgement was *stifling.*

And while the word judgement stood out in my mind, it was part of a much grander energy ingrained in all humanity — *resistance.*

This is what it felt like to go against creation, against what *is.* The feeling of resistance was choking me, closing my airway, and suffocating my life force.

If something wasn't meant to exist in the world, it wouldn't. Yet here we are, deciding what does and doesn't belong. Resisting and wanting to *uncreate* the creation of others. Resistance takes an enormous amount of energy. *Our energy.*

Higher vibrational states like acceptance, gratitude, and peace are all energies that add love to our experience of life. They expand us and expand those around us, allowing life to pass through, effortlessly.

These expansive emotions lighten us up. *Resistance closes us down.* We often complain about how challenging life can be. When we accept all things, life becomes easy. Fighting is what makes it difficult.

We resist life in many ways, some as grandiose as protests, and some as subtle as judgement. And we're remarkably clever at disguising our judgements. Outright condemnation is easy to spot, but opinions, criticisms, beliefs, and even casual observations can carry the same energy. The wrapper changes. The energy doesn't.

Personally, I was no stranger to the walls of judgement, but I wasn't seeing them for what they were. I didn't see myself as judgemental because it often came out as constructive criticism — what I believed was helpful. But I never looked at it from the other side. What I considered useful advice and correcting mistakes, others heard as harsh criticism and judgement, often triggering a feeling that they weren't good enough.

I understood why I built barriers against certain energies, like hate and anger. I understood their effects on me and my projection onto the world. It all made so much sense, but it hadn't occurred to me that criticism was having the same effect. It was blocking the flow of creation.

A judgement is a wall. The moment we judge something, deciding it doesn't belong or that it shouldn't exist, we stop its energy from passing through. We not only block it in our own lives, we try to block it in the lives of others, encroaching on their free will and their own journey.

Judgements are defense mechanisms, born from survival instincts rooted in fear. We judge what triggers us. And what triggers us is almost always a response to energy that we've trapped within ourselves. Something we're afraid to feel.

The more we resist something, the more draining it becomes. The harder we push against what is, the more it pushes back, fighting for its right to exist. Good, bad, indifferent — energy just is. And the denser our walls of resistance, the more of our own life force it takes to keep those walls enforced. But it doesn't have to be that way.

We can believe something is good, without something else needing to be bad. If something feels right to you, it doesn't mean something else has to be wrong. We all have preferences, but we can prefer something without judging anything else. It's all in *how* we go about it.

It's time to understand there's no such thing as right or wrong when it comes to creation. Our reality is simply a manifestation of the energy creating an experience. When we encounter an aspect of creation we don't like, we're meant to create an alternative. Not judge it. Not fight it.

When we meet a contradicting belief or opposing energy with resistance, we collide. It's like two rocks facing off. They chip away at each other, blocking one another, stopping the flow of life. Throughout the evening, the states of matter kept returning as the perfect illustration. They were continually showing me what it means to be dense, to live more fluidly, and ultimately, to become as light as air.

A rock is solid. Dense. Impenetrable. Its particles packed tightly together, leaving no room for anything to move through. When two rocks hit: Crash. Fracture. Damage. Their particles can't commingle or intertwine. Neither experiences the other except from the surface. They just hit each other and stop.

Water is lighter. Fluid. Things can move through it and flow with it. Two liquids can merge, becoming something new. Their particles are looser, more welcoming. We can make waves and swim through liquids, but we still feel resistance. Less dense than a solid, and not as free as a gas.

And then there's air. Its gaseous particles are so expanded, so spaced out, that any other matter simply passes through. No collision. No resistance. No damage. Just a quick commingling, experiencing each other, and moving on.

If we lighten up, expanding our energy and giving our particles space, there's no clash. No bang. There's no sound when a rock hits the air. The air just allows the rock to pass through and goes on its merry way.

When we're like the gas, we allow what is to pass through with ease. When we lighten up our beliefs, we accept creation and allow all to pass through freely, including anything we label as dark, evil, or dense.

The more we fight the world, the more the world fights back. Regardless of whether we're putting energy into creating something or stopping something, we're still feeding its energy. Fighting only compounds our own density.

And yet we continue resisting, reacting to things we see, hear, touch, taste, or smell. Any sense can trigger a reaction. But most often, we react to other people — their ideas, words, and actions. Why?

When we talk about something not resonating with us, it's a figure of speech, but also science. It's a vibrational mis-match. And that only means one thing, quite literally: It has a higher or lower frequency than our own.

That alone is no cause for judgement, because frequency just is. Letting things pass through is effortless. So if we are reacting to something, if we are judging something, we are resisting it. We are trying to stop it because it's different. Because it doesn't match our own vibrational state.

And when things are different, we're often afraid of them. Things that are lower vibration we judge as wrong, convinced of our own righteousness. And things that are a higher vibration, we'll often judge when we have an insecurity that we'll never reach that vibration.

And if we've refused to experience it, if we stopped it from passing through, all we've done is held it captive in the present moment. Most of us approach life with good intentions. We believe that if we resist something, if we fight something, we're doing the world a favor. In vibrational truth, the harder we resist, *the more of it we re-create.*

That was one of the biggest lessons here for me. We only have the present moment, and all of creation is passing through it one experience at a time. Only the human ego would try to stop creation. Ever hear the phrase, "This too shall pass"? Not if we're blocking it. Not if we're holding it hostage.

A new vision emerged with unmistakable force. Once again the energy was so strong, I fully embodied it. I found myself standing tall and proud, physically mimicking the stance in my vision. I was armored from head to toe — a literal knight in shining armor. Drawing my sword, I prepared to fight. With my other arm, I raised up my shield in a gallant effort to protect myself, and called out, "I am ready to fight evil!"

A glorious righteousness coursed through my body. I felt larger than life, ready to save the world from all the evils in it. But this heroic energy only lasted a moment. I was quickly deflated by a whisper from this deeper wisdom of life. *You didn't come here to fight evil.*

I have several good friends who feel guided to be the light, fighting against the darkness. I understand that calling deeply. But the message coming through in that moment was unmistakable: *Fighting anything is resisting a part of creation.*

In my vision, I released my sword and shield, letting them fall to the ground. My armor disappeared, and once again the energy compelled me to speak, and I called out, "You didn't come here to fight anything!"

The messages continued, even stronger.

The warrior souls in this life, still carrying the warring energy of the past, misunderstood the assignment. They showed up armored and ready for battle, declaring, "I am here to stop evil!" But life keeps trying to tell them: *That's not it.*

We're not here to stop evil, we're here to experience it. To know it. To understand it from the inside. That's the only way to allow it to move on. We choose where to pour our energy — creating more of what we want, or draining it fighting what we resist.

Until now, the messages were focused on restoring our energy in the present moment. When it came to evil, the channeling dove deeper, and for the first time, into past lives.

If you're still carrying a righteous sword, swinging it against the darkness, and telling everyone how much injustice and evil still exists, consider this: *You were evil.* You were the darkness you're now so determined to vanquish.

I'll give you a moment with that one. When it came through, I felt the power it held to shift perspectives on an entirely new level — if we allow it to. I began feeling into how many people might reject this message, even judge it. It's bold enough saying not to stop evil and allow it to exist. And now I'm telling people that *they were evil* in a past life?

A small window into reincarnation had cracked open, one that future channelings would dive deeper into. The wisdom was adamant. This existence is about experiencing *all of creation.*

And if the point of life is to experience all that creation has to offer, we would *have to* live more than one lifetime here.

Our souls come back again and again to experience all aspects of creation, from every angle, becoming intimately tied to all that life has to offer — male and female, the hero and the villain, the savior and the demon.

Simple Truth: We didn't come into this reality to fight anything. We came here to experience everything.

We live through various aspects of life so we'll know them fully, so we'll understand what it's like and why it exists. And then we come back to life on Earth with an inner recognition of that aspect of life we previously lived. Not to resist it, but to have compassion for it. To *accept* it without judgement to help *free* it. Because we *were* it.

Through our lifetimes, we're meant to learn how someone becomes so loved or so feared. And in our present life, we can say: *I was there. I understand, and I don't need to live it again. Now I allow it to pass through, and I choose something new.* And gradually, lifetime by lifetime as we lighten up, our judgements soften, our beliefs loosen, and our righteousness fades.

The next time you get the urge to complain, judge, or fight the darkness, remember this: The only time we see darkness in the world is when there isn't enough light. The more density we carry and the more walls we have up, the less of our light shines out, dimming our ability to illuminate the world around us. We're the only ones who can unblock ourselves. The only ones who can let more of our light shine into the world.

And since we can't uncreate what is, how do we stop the urge to judge something we feel is wrong?

We bring awareness to the fact that all things in creation belong. That we are not victims of creation, but hold the power of choice. If we don't like something, whether it's a song, a movie, a religion, a government, or a leader, it's not about judging them. It's simply about experiencing the energy and deciding if we'd rather experience something different.

The only job we have as creators is focusing on creating something new, not resisting what is.

We need to learn to see things energetically, as different frequencies and vibrations. When we do, we shift out of judgement into acceptance, and our vibration literally rises.

We can be in the same amount of wonder admiring the dense walls of a gorge as much as the river flowing through it. The water is a higher vibrational state of matter than the rock, but that doesn't make the rock worse or the river better. The river doesn't criticize, insult, or belittle the rocks for being a different state of matter. And the water isn't jealous of the air for being lighter.

All of life on Earth accepts the state it's in without judging the state of others — except humans. And while we're the only ones who can change our energetic state, we often choose not to, playing victim to our circumstances instead.

The fastest way to change the world is to pour our collective power and intention into what we want to create, not what we want to destroy. Humanity gets caught up in itself when we think we have to stop one thing to create something else. As we bring more awareness into our consciousness and learn to lighten up, we'll finally free ourselves of the dense energy of resistance.

Imagine every judgement as a rock sitting on the roadway of collective creation. Every belief and stereotype we hold onto becomes a boulder. Gay is wrong. Women are weak. The rich are corrupt. Piling up until we can no longer continue on our path of creation.

Every judgement is resistance. It creates a block, hardening us every time we resist. So let's become more aware of our criticisms and judgements and see them for what they actually are: invitations. They're calling us to see something within that we're afraid to admit, to feel, to accept — something that needs to be freed.

So next time you find yourself judging something, pause and ask, *Why am I not okay with this? What am I really resisting? What about this frightens me?*

A powerful reminder echoed in my mind: *You came here to experience all of it, lighten up, and let it pass through.*

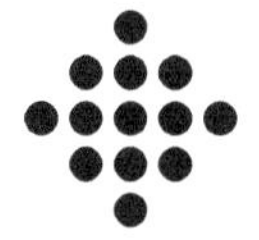

PART 3

The Soul's Choice

Revelation after revelation had poured into my awareness. I felt the weight of fear. The gravity of trauma. I understood the walls we built and why we're not here to resist creation. Now it was time to dive deeper into our soul's choice to be here. I found myself asking: *Why do we wish to experience such a dense reality?*

For a long time, I've believed our soul makes many vital choices from the other side before it incarnates. It not only chooses to experience human life, it chooses the lessons to learn and the karma to clear. It even chooses the family to be birthed into, down to the date and time.

The thought that we would consciously choose, before birth, to take on trauma in our upcoming life can be a controversial idea. To those who were abused and are still healing, it can bring up feelings such as anger, confusion, and much more. To accept the possibility that some part of ourselves would choose suffering seems maddening from our human perspective. After all, would you bring children into this life planning to traumatize them?

Yet the belief that our soul plans its life is widely held in the spiritual community. But the explanation rarely goes deeper than simply saying: *Our souls have lessons to learn and contracts to fill* — as though becoming human was some kind of masochistic assignment we signed up for.

So if it's true, that we plan our lives here, the real question is: *Why?* If our free will extends to the other side before we're born, why would we freely choose so much suffering? So much pain? So much density?

Why would we choose this?

CHAPTER 7:

The Lost Innocence of Youth

Throughout the challenges of our life, we've hardened our energy, shut down emotionally, and buried our emotional wounds. And here we are, carrying the weight of what it means to be human. But we aren't created this way.

I felt myself slipping back into the energy of youth, before any emotional wounding. I was feeling the joy and innocence that accompanies childhood.

Children arrive as clear vessels: innocent, present, and full of wonder. They're open, alive with joy, and eager to experience life in the realm of the senses. Their energy is light and expansive, welcoming all frequencies, all vibrations, all colors of the rainbow. They don't judge the world. They experience it. They let energy pass through them the way it was always meant to move.

This isn't just innocence. This is the natural state of life itself. Children know something we've forgotten — that life is meant to flow.

The freedom of childhood comes from greeting the world with arms, heart, and mind wide open. Children are unjaded by creation, familial expectations, political mandates, or religious dogma. They greet life with wonder and curiosity. Their energy is vibrant and free-flowing, unencumbered by the layers of judgement and fear that weigh down adults.

This childlike state of being isn't something we lose as we grow older. It's something we bury beneath an avalanche of density as the expectations and demands of the world slowly weigh us down.

And then life begins to teach us, not how to flow, but how to defend.

As helpless infants in the physical world, we learn through observation, absorbing life energetically. We mimic the examples shown to us, beginning with our parents. Not all learning comes in positive forms. Pain is often one of the greatest teachers. But when we don't understand pain through the eyes of awareness, we become afraid of it. And fear of pain is what builds our first walls.

As children, we absorb what's modeled around us, healthy or harmful. If we were never shown how to release trapped energy, we learn a different pattern: take on trauma and density, bury it, and blame others instead of healing it.

We were meant to learn from our emotional pain, shift our understanding, and move on — not cling to our mistakes, regret our choices, or resent our lessons and teachers. We weren't meant to carry our density forward as our identity.

Without guidance, we repeat what we see. We build walls just as our parents built theirs. We carry the same burdens, mistaking their projections as our own flaws. The cycle continues, not because we are broken or damaged, but because no one taught us any other way.

An unhealed parent carries their own traumas. When triggered by their child, they burst: scolding, yelling, demeaning. A barrage of dense, unhealed pain lands on an innocent child who has no framework to understand what's happening.

The child interprets it personally. They believe they caused the anger. That they deserved it. And so the trauma is incorrectly internalized, creating a trauma point in that child's energy field.

That child's energy shifts, thickens, densifies. The force field goes up. The open, welcoming child who once let everything pass through eventually becomes a hardened adult.

And the cycle of reaction over response continues. Ignorance over awareness. We forget the nature of life: experience, release, expand, and allow energy to flow.

If we were taught to let experiences go and allow energy to pass through, we would view life for what it truly is: a string of experiences here to help us choose the creation we want to experience more of. We would grow up without accumulating trauma. And as we consciously choose the experiences we prefer, we tune ourselves to those frequencies, attracting more of what we want.

But instead of being raised as creators of life, we're conditioned to believe we're victims of it. We're taught to react. To survive. To obey. We're not shown how to release pain or transmute our negative experiences into wisdom.

We are born free — limitless, connected, and alive. We aren't born with blocks, or walls, or judgement. We build them, because that's the example we're shown.

Simple Truth: We live as though creation is happening to us, forgetting that it's actually flowing through us.

And when we live as victims, fear becomes our compass, guiding us into even more density. And who does fear enslave? Those who are not aware. The ones disconnected from their being, from source, from the universe. Connection requires openness and expansiveness. When we're closed down, hardened, and afraid, it becomes almost impossible to hear the calling of our soul.

I felt it without a shadow of a doubt. As a soul between lives, we know precisely what we are getting ourselves into by incarnating on Earth. We choose it freely.

But the grand question still lingered.

If all this is true, if we know we are coming into a life of density, pain, and trauma, *why would we choose this?* If part of becoming human means signing up for suffering, why would we incarnate?

These are the kinds of questions every traumatized human asks, including myself. And the answers that were about to be revealed would shift everything I thought I knew — not just my understanding of why we choose to be human, but my understanding of what it means to be a parent, and more importantly, a child.

CHAPTER 8:

The Heroic Role of Children

Abuse often flows to those closest to us. And while there is much abuse from lovers, bosses, or even strangers, for many of us, it's our own families who create the majority of fear, suffering, and chaos in our lives.

Believing in something is not the same as understanding it. For a long time, I've believed that we *choose* our family, but I didn't fully *understand* it, especially when thinking of those born into abusive homes. Fully embracing the concept that we choose our families, along with all the pain and density that accompanies that life, honestly sounded a bit deranged.

There had to be a reason our souls would take on such a life.

For hours, a core message had been programmed into my being — *energy has to move*. It was no surprise the answer once again related to releasing energy and was delivered with profound love.

We didn't come here to be victims to trauma. We came to release it.

Really allow that to sink in. We didn't come here to be *victims* to trauma. We came to *release* it. But in order to release it, we *have to* experience it first. We have to take it on in order to let it go, so we can release humanity from its own prison and stop the cycle of trauma once and for all.

Before we incarnate, our soul exists outside the confines of time and space. And we don't arrive randomly. We *volunteer.* Our soul *chooses* the family and circumstances with purpose, every energetic detail. From a specific body carrying specific genes to the astrological moment of entry — all to set the stage for lessons, growth, and a core mission of *restoring the flow of life.*

We can't uncreate the trauma of the past, but we can come back to Earth to free it. We are here to move what has been stuck and unblock what has been dammed, sometimes for generations.

Simple Truth: We take on trauma in order to release it.

From the other side, the soul sees everything, including the full energetic map. The patterns. The pain. All the places where our life force has been blocked for decades, maybe centuries. It sees the generational trauma, the familial wounds — *and the potential.* The immense opportunity for healing. It sees it all, without distortion, without the fog of fear.

From the other side, we understand. We see our parents clearly. The density they're carrying, the stuck energy, the walls they built, the black holes slowly draining their life force. We see all of it from a place of understanding, without judgement. From a place of unconditional love.

We know that somewhere along the way, our family took on too much. They got weighed down by density and covered too much of their light. They forgot who they were and why they were really here. They forgot to remain open, to remain light, to allow life to pass through — so we came to remind them.

Our parents had the same assignment that's now passed on to us: come in, free the energy, experience all life has to offer, and keep creating. So our soul makes its choice, not only for the lessons we will face, but for the *healing we will offer.*

One of the bravest roles in the universe is to become human again. We take on life knowing we have the opportunity to unclog the arteries of our lineage, dammed up by generations of density. With all the love that exists on the other side, the soul whispers: *Hold on. I am coming in to help.*

The soul descends. A child is born, drawing its first breath of life, still connected with the truth of why it came. Our very presence is a catalyst. And this is where our soul's mission begins, at home.

Children incarnate not only to experience life on Earth, but to reflect truth. To offer a glint of light and spark the memory in their parents of who they were before the density took hold. Children arrive in all their innocence. Still connected to source, light as air, and instinctively see where the energy is blocked.

And from that point of clarity, children see things the parents can't. They know, without words, without even understanding how they know, *exactly* where the parents are holding on tightest.

We marvel at how a child can prod at precisely the right, or the wrong, place. They seem to know, with supernatural precision, which button to push, wound to poke, and wall to knock on. It isn't an accident.

It's the assignment. It's the agreement made outside of time, before any of us descend into the density of Earth. The child is an energetic alert system. A cosmic finger pointing directly at the parents' blockages.

Just as physical pain tells us where the body needs healing, children tell the parents where their energy needs freeing. And often acting intuitively, kids follow the clear guidance of their soul. They come knocking, trying to break down their parents' walls.

I envisioned myself as a child once again. This time, I was acting out this gripping journey of the soul incarnating, choosing to come in to help their parents free their lineage. This may have been the most profound message of the night — the culmination of everything I was shown throughout the evening. I stood there pointing, poking the air, saying, "Here. *Right here.* This is where the energy is stuck. This is what needs to move. This is why I am here."

But the parents, misunderstanding that children are life's messengers, don't respond with love. Instead, the parents condemn the child for going against their will and beliefs, *often punishing the child for it.*

Not because they don't love their child. But because their density has blinded them to the truth. Their own energy has become so thick, so calcified around their trauma points, they've lost touch with their true essence. Their own light. The fear of facing and feeling their own traumas, even for the sake of their children, outweighs the thought of releasing it.

So the child reaches out lovingly, trying to get the parents' attention, trying to release the blockage — to restore the flow of life. *I'm just trying to help,* the child's soul whispers. *I'm going to unclog the energy as gently as I can.*

The parent unconsciously swats the child's hand away. *Don't touch it. Don't touch my blocked energy. It's mine.*

They don't even know they're doing it. And so their pain continually bangs at the door until it finds a way out — unleashed onto the child in one form or another. Not because the parent lacks love, but because they lack the awareness to face what they're afraid to feel. Real strength isn't holding on to pain. It's having the courage to release it.

That's the tragedy of unconscious protection. The very walls built to keep out the pain of the world, keep out the healing, too.

The energy of the child's soul crying out in desperation overwhelmed me as this scene continued to play out. My heart pounded. My eyes filled with tears. And I called out with more emotion and love than I've ever felt, voicing the words of the child.

"Mom, Dad, you don't understand. It's hurting you. The energy is stuck. The pressure is building. I'm trying to unclog the energy. You're stopping the flow. You're holding it too tight. You're reversing the flow of life. You're going to die. *Please! Let it go!*"

The child cries out over and over to the parents, begging them to release the trauma. Triggered, the parents continue to react out of fear, instead of responding from awareness, adding density to themselves and their child.

We come in with the possibility that our very birth may be the catalyst that frees our parents' blockages and finally allows them to release it all. But we also come in knowing the other possibility: They'll not only hold onto their density — they'll pass it on.

So the child makes one last plea. "I'm trying to save you. It has weighed you down for too long. Can't you see it's draining you? *Can't you see it's killing you?* Please let it go. *Please!*"

But our parents were never taught how to release it, so they hold on even tighter. They build their walls even taller, believing they're protecting themselves and their child from their pain — not understanding that the child is here to help free them from it.

The child, this soul of light, keeps trying to free the blockage and can't. Because you cannot grab density with light. You cannot move a boulder with a breeze. Only density can move density.

If our parents are not ready to heal, they'll continue to deflect their trauma. So we bravely do whatever it takes to move the energy, even if it means taking on the burden ourselves.

The child cannot stand by watching the parents continue to harden. And once all the attempts to point out the blocks fail, the child makes a choice. An ultimate sacrifice. A true act of love.

To get a grip on the blockage, the child takes on density in order to move it. The soul knows if it takes on too much, it may never release it, but it's worth the risk. And as the density accumulates, the openness closes. The lightness dims. And the child shares their parents' pain. Not because the child was forced to bear it. *Because the child had to take on the energy in an attempt to release what their parents couldn't.*

We sacrifice our innocence so the density will be in our hands. We give ourselves the power to release it, making it our choice to stop the cycle — for all humanity.

I could no longer bear the energy of witnessing this emotional exchange. I called out with passion, once again giving voice to the child's soul. "You couldn't bear this weight yourself, and it's okay. You do not have to carry this density alone. It's crushing you. Let me help you carry it. Let me release it."

The black holes of trauma carry an enormous amount of energy, and so it takes an even larger amount of energy to break free of them. The density building up inside humanity has been building for millennia. It cannot be undone in one life. So the energy is freed over lifetimes and generations.

And on the other side, the angels bow down.

They whisper in our ear, *We honor you for coming in. For taking on the pain. For carrying the cross for all those who came before you.*

My vision shifted and I was no longer the child. I was now seeing generations of a family standing in a line, pulling something. The youngest members, the newest souls to incarnate, were at the end. They were surrounded by other souls, watching, cheering them on. The accumulated fear, trauma, and abuse of all the generations was a giant plug preventing the water of life from flowing. There was a metal loop attached to the back of the plug, and a long chain attached to that, which the souls were gripping.

Their hands clutched the chain, pulling at it with all their might, like a tug of war. They were trying to release the density of their lineage. But the block was too strong. The pressure building was too great.

One child, one lifetime, wasn't strong enough to release it. It had built up for too long. So more generations of children had come in, each generation helping to loosen the plug, moving it just a bit, but not enough.

So they cried out in unison, "Send in the next generation. We're loosening it."

And another soul volunteers. Another child is born into the lineage. Standing next to its ancestors, it picks up the chain, and together they all pull, loosening it even more. Generation after generation, each one pulls, taking on density to move the energy, to counter the weight of the blockage. Each generation loosening it a little more.

And one day when enough love, sacrifice, and awareness has poured in — *pop!*

The plug pulls free. The energy of creation begins flowing again, and humanity can embrace its true potential and power.

And the angels cheer, knowing it was not in vain. Knowing we would succeed in our mission. Knowing that each generation lightens the load and lessens the burden of the previous one.

This is what every child has chosen. What we have chosen. The weight we carry, the pain that hardens us — it isn't punishment. *It is purpose.*

We came in knowing what it would cost, *and we came anyway.* Our souls proclaimed, "I don't *want* to take on trauma, *but I will.* I will make that sacrifice to free humanity from its pain."

We came to loosen the plug another inch. Or maybe, just maybe, we'll be the ones who finally set it free.

This is the heroic role of every child. Done out of love for every parent. I collapsed to my knees in tears as I fully embraced these final insights.

And our parents? The ones who passed on their pain? They were once children as well. Their souls made the same choice ours did. To jump into the void of creation. To sacrifice their light as the child to their parents' density, our grandparents.

This is the cycle of life. And the cycle ends when someone has enough insight and courage to see it — and chooses to no longer carry the pain. Chooses to bring light to the darkness. And is brave enough to face the trauma and lighten up enough to finally set it free.

So now I ask you: *Are you the one?*

The End of My Journey and The Beginning of Yours

It began with five words: *How do I release fear?*

One simple question, set with intention, cracked open something I never would have anticipated. Hours of channeled visions, energy, and revelations had poured through me, building step by step, guiding me toward something larger. As each layer was peeled back, another was revealed, expanding my being from the core.

And then as suddenly as it had begun, it was over. As the energy settled, the last words of the channeling gently came through me, spoken softly:

"And now it's up to you. If you want to be the wall, if you want to be the diamond, if you want to be the black hole—or if you understand the assignment that you need to lighten up. You need to let it go. You need to let it flow. Tonight was about releasing fear and letting go. Thank you, and good night."

Still standing there, I fell silent. I slowly opened my eyes, giving them a moment to adjust. I was in awe. Humbled. Stunned.

I looked at my wife. Heart racing. Mind blown wide open. "Did that just happen?"

"Yeah it did!" she enthusiastically replied, returning a look of astonishment.

"I can't believe it," I mumbled, still in shock.

I took a long breath, trying to settle everything that was still pulsating through me. "That was incredible. I can't believe… I can't believe I didn't record that!" I exclaimed with a mix of disappointment and enthusiasm.

"Good thing I did!" my wife responded with a big smile. "That was pure gold. As soon as you started talking, I knew this was something magical."

"Thank God!" I let out a loud exhale. My whole body felt electrified. The adrenaline was still pumping. I started pacing around the room, taking in everything that just transpired.

I was astonished at how profound, and yet how simple, it was presented. Only one question now remained, which I voiced to my wife. "Now what?"

What was I to do with all of this insight? I felt an urgency to immediately share it with everyone I knew, to shout it from the rooftops. But then what? What would people do with it? Would it bring them peace, or more questions? Questions I wasn't sure I had answers to — yet.

It was my wife who brought me back to Earth. "Don't rush it," she said. "Let it sink in. Give yourself time to integrate it all."

She was right. She usually is.

Still in disbelief, I sat down and tried to process it all. Allowing. Breathing. Integrating. Some deeper part of me fully recognized the significance of what happened — the gravity of it all. When we finally went to bed, it was still settling into my being. But the question still burned in my mind.

Now what?

Now I understood more about life. About energy. About humanity. And it was time to integrate it. To live it. To become it.

And now I pass it to you, to continue on your path of expansion. But our journey together isn't finished just yet...

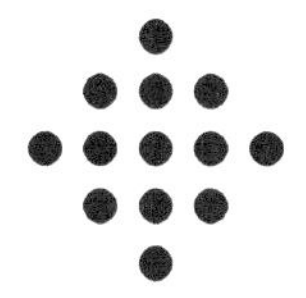

PART 4

Restoring the Flow

We can carry the most profound spiritual understanding in our minds while remaining completely stuck in our energy. When we're stuck in our own density, it's like running through mud. Creation keeps moving — evolving, expanding, reaching toward what's next while we feel held back, wondering why life seems like it's passing us by.

When professional race car drivers have worn tires, they know it's time for a pit stop. Stopping takes valuable time. It means falling behind while the new tires are put on, but then they'll return to the race with fresh tires, ready to make up ground.

Many of us continue the race of life on worn tires, some even with flat tires, because we don't want to take the time to repair ourselves, to refuel, to change the tires. Not only does it slow us down, it causes permanent damage to our vehicle. And yet we race on, blaming the road, blaming the vehicle, thinking we'll fall behind if we stop to take care of what's slowing us down. As we lose momentum, we're not just losing the race. We may never finish it.

It's time to pull over. Change the tires. Refuel. And get back in the race. It's time to shake off the mud, bring down the walls, and rediscover just how bright we can shine.

This is where the real work begins. It doesn't have to be *hard* work, but it has to be *honest* work. The kind that asks us to stop hiding from ourselves, blaming the world around us, and finally put down what we've been carrying.

Density slows the flow of life. Barriers block it. Trauma reverses it. It's time to lower the walls and allow life to move through us the way it was meant to. We are here to restore the flow. Not someday. Right now.

It's time to lighten up!

CHAPTER 9:

Stop Passing On the Pain

The next day I was still in shock.

Shocked that I had just channeled for three hours. Shocked at the beauty and simplicity of what came through. Shocked that it came *through me*. As I continued to integrate this powerful journey, another message emerged: *It's time to stop passing on the pain.*

Years, decades, and generations of accumulated energy, trauma, and pain run deep. Lightening our compounded density takes time, patience, and dedication. And while the task of helping the world release its trauma and lighten up can feel next to impossible, we only need to take it one step at a time.

Not all steps are leaps. Some are barely noticeable, cracking the door open just enough to let a sliver of light in. That's all we need. Creating even a small space helps the energy move, allows awareness in, and begins the process of healing.

When we incarnate, our soul doesn't arrive with judgement or carry resentment for the mission it's taking on. We come in with love and understanding, knowing that our parents made the same choice. Knowing that we might take on suffering.

Pain is passed on when it's left unprocessed and unhealed. Even though our pain is often deflected onto those we're closest with, when we carry unhealed pain, it can affect everyone in our lives. And we are the only ones who can break the cycle.

It's up to us to stop the downward spiral into more density. We didn't come into this life to be abused, blame others for what they passed on, or take on shame for accepting it. The cycle of pain wasn't born from cruelty. It was the result of energy being blocked and will perpetuate out of necessity until the flow of creation is restored. Our parents did their best even if we have a difficult time accepting it. We're all doing the best we can. And now it's up to us to decide if we want to lighten up and heal our trauma, pain, and fear — or continue to pass it on.

Ever play *hot potato*? Let's delve into the origin of this children's game and look at how much wisdom it holds.

We're gathered in a kitchen with friends and family. The timer dings. The baked potatoes are ready and taken out of the oven. You grab one, and it burns. The pain is immediate. You quite literally can't handle it.

So you toss it to the person closest to you to see if they can stand the pain you couldn't. That person instinctively reaches out to save it, not even thinking about getting burned. They were just next in line.

If it is still too hot for them, they have the same reaction. *It's too painful to hold, so I'll pass it on.*

And that's what we do with painful emotions and trauma. We don't want to feel the pain, so we pass it to someone else.

But there's another layer. As the potato gets passed from person to person, it cools. It no longer burns, but it's still uncomfortable to hold. Now we have a choice: pass it on again or accept the discomfort, saving someone else the pain.

I love that a children's game, passed on for generations, demonstrates so clearly what we do with our pain. If any of us actually picked up a scorching hot potato, we'd drop it immediately. Pure reflex. We wouldn't really toss it to someone, knowing it would burn them.

Let's go deeper still.

You use tongs to toss a scorching hot potato to someone you care about: a child, a spouse, a sibling. You look at them and yell, "Catch!" They instinctively reach out their hands, trusting you completely, and catch it — because why would you deliberately hurt them?

Would you really do that knowing it would burn them?

Of course not. Not intentionally. And yet we do this almost every day. We pass on the pain. Not because we're monsters. Because we're holding something we can't bear, and no one ever showed us how to handle it. No one ever taught us how to safely release it without hurting someone else.

Follow me one last time.

Imagine there's a child who can't feel physical pain in their hands. They catch the scorching potato that their parent throws at them. They don't know that they should release it. Holding it as it sears their skin, it causes permanent damage and scars their hands for life. Now imagine that parent repeatedly burns the child every day, sometimes several times a day, compounding the wounds and never allowing the skin to heal.

I'm guessing that's a vivid enough scenario.

If this actually happened to a child you knew, you'd have that parent in jail instantly, saving the child from repeated abuse. And while we take physical child abuse very seriously, we allow ourselves to emotionally abuse our children every day that we pass on our unhealed pain.

This is why generational trauma perpetuates. This is why abused parents so often abuse their children. This is why patterns repeat across decades, bloodlines, and history. It isn't fate. It isn't inevitable. It's energy that was deflected instead of released. Passed on instead of passed through.

And our solution as a society? Punish the abuser instead of trying to heal them, instead of releasing the black hole that's tearing them apart. Hurt people hurt people. It's not a judgement. It's physics.

And while it feels devastatingly personal to the person receiving abuse, the person passing it on isn't *seeing you* — they're *seeing an outlet for their pain.*

When we don't face, feel, understand, and release our trauma, we become it, embodying the energy trapped within us. When we don't heal anger, we become angry. When we don't heal abandonment, we abandon. What we don't heal, we hand down.

Some of us will deflect until the day we die. But some part of us always knows, and always feels, the moment we harm another. When our own pain runs deep enough, it overrides everything, including our instinct to protect the ones we love most, even our own children.

Regardless of how good or bad of a job our parents did protecting us, they did their best with the density they carried. But what if we have parenting all wrong? What if what's needed isn't protection but awareness? The kind that helps them understand why adults react the way they do, and teaches them to release what was passed on.

And whether we have children or not, we pass it on to friends, siblings, partners, and anyone who triggers us. *Somehow, causing someone else pain has become more acceptable than taking responsibility for it.*

Most of it happens without a single moment of awareness, without realizing just how deep we're hurting the people we love and hurting the world. When we can't address our own pain, we often pass it on, carrying shame and guilt over how we treated others. We rationalize, deflect, and blame. And another dark, spiraling black hole of density grows within us.

We all feel this happening, but we aren't equipped to handle it. We're desperately crying out for help while our own density muffles the answers that have been right in front of us. It's why this material struck me so deeply. It points to the way out. The way forward. The way through.

To believe someone needs protection, we have to believe they're in danger. And living in that belief means living in fear, in survival mode, draining our nervous system, instead of feeding it. We condense ourselves when living in fear, and we condense others by teaching them fear. We build these walls of density, shutting out experiences, words, thoughts, images, music — where does fear end?

We spend over a decade of our childhood learning math, history, science, you name it, and yet we have no model for letting go of our fear and trauma. We learn about atoms, gravity, and electricity. But no one realizes the most important and personal form of energy to learn about is *our* energy. Our trapped emotions. So it isn't instinctive for any of us to release emotional pain — it's instinctive to pass it on.

The power to break the cycle is in our hands. It's time to own it. To trust ourselves to take responsibility for it, even if it wasn't ours to begin with. Now it's our turn to do what it takes to stop passing on the pain.

This wisdom came through to bring understanding that trauma is passed on, *not because we deserve it*, but because *others never released it*. This is about choosing *empowerment* over victimhood.

Just as this channeling gave me awareness, it's now given to you. We break the cycle by making a conscious choice to *pass on awareness instead of pain*. That's how we help the world heal. That's how we help it lighten up.

Set a desire for change. Begin the process of lightening the density, if only a little each day. Lighten the places where you feel stuck, in pain, or where you've been told you're broken.

Bring awareness to every interaction you have with family, friends, and strangers. If you're feeling triggered, remember this wisdom, pause, and ask yourself: "What is this showing me? What fear do I need to release?"

Simple Truth: Pain is passed on from one generation to the next until someone is aware enough to choose differently.

We've all felt things heating up whether there's a confrontation building, a relationship under pressure, or two opposing beliefs about to ignite. Most of us interpret that heat as a sign everything is going wrong. Typically, our instinct is to either explode or retreat. But like triggers, what if the heat was helping us?

Think about what heat does. It activates. It transforms. Water becomes steam. A blowtorch doesn't destroy a wall — it dissolves it, turning density into flow. When things heat up inside us, that's energy trying to release. Trying to move. Trying to break through walls that have been standing for years, even generations.

The boiling point isn't the end. It's the point of transformation.

Next time things heat up, bring awareness to the situation. Do you want to be the volcano exploding outward and passing on the pain? Or recognize the heat for what it is: energy asking to be released. Next time, allow it to move through you rather than deflecting it onto someone else.

I'm not here to say this is easy.

If it was, you wouldn't be reading this book. Some have carried so much weight that it would bring anyone to their knees. Some have been through things no human being should ever experience. And for those who felt it was too much, who broke under the weight — I understand. So many of us understand. *You were not meant to carry so much alone.* My hope is for this material to shine a light at the end of that dark tunnel.

The pain we were born into wasn't ours. It was passed on by someone who couldn't release it, someone who received it from another. All the way back. Generation after generation. We are part of an unbroken chain, trying to survive something we were never taught how to release, because we never really understood why it happened.

And now it's our turn.

It's our turn to understand this life. To understand why our soul chose to take this on. We did not come here to be victims. We did not fall into density to become more dense. We came here to lighten it up. And enlighten the world along the way.

We have the power to break the cycle. To release the dam. Not because we're stronger than everyone who came before us, but because we're more *aware*. Awareness changes everything. Awareness is the beginning of all healing.

Every generation has a choice. And every one of us has a choice.

It doesn't require perfection. It doesn't require having it all figured out, processing every wound, clearing every pattern, healing every scar. It only requires one step at a time. When blinded by pain and fear, we live from reaction. Once we become aware, there's no going back. Every decision moving forward becomes a *conscious choice*. And every day we have the opportunity to choose to live differently. Live more aware. Live lighter.

Choose to break the cycle. *Choose* to stop passing on the pain. Once you make the choice to face your density and release it, the road to freedom is clear.

Tell yourself today, and every day: *I will no longer pass on my pain*. It's not the whole journey, but it's a huge step. Awareness lights the torch. Intention leads the way. And healing follows, in whatever form it needs to take.

Allow all of this material to fully sink in. What will follow is compassion. Compassion for your parents. For those who hurt you. For those you have hurt. And most of all, for yourself.

Our parents' lives were likely harder than ours. And their parents' lives were harder than theirs. Each generation moves the energy — taking on some weight, lightening a little more, passing on a little less. Slowly. Imperfectly. But the energy moves. It lightens. And on some level, the soul always remembers its mission: Free the density and allow creation to continue in the direction of expansion.

Each generation comes in more expanded than the last. They come into a lighter world than their parents did, allowing more light into their being, allowing them to shine more light into the world.

Even the most painful childhoods moved energy forward. Even parents who seemed to fail completely still changed the density of the lineage. And even if it was only by a fraction — that fraction matters. That fraction is why you're here, reading these words, aware enough to choose something different.

This isn't about excusing anyone. It's about understanding. About seeing those who caused pain as people lost in their own density, doing the only thing they knew. They didn't have this information. They didn't have this awareness. They weren't taught to stop passing on the pain.

That changes now.

The torch is yours. What you do with it changes not just your life, but ripples into the lives of every person you know, including your lineage, forward and back. True healing is energetic, and it doesn't just free you. It heals the collective.

It's never too late to stop passing on the pain, judgement, drama, and hate. Not all at once. One choice at a time.

The cycle ends when someone decides it does.

So I ask: *Are you ready to stop passing on the pain?*

CHAPTER 10:

Reclaiming Your True Self

A few days after the channeling, I was talking with my good friend, Barry. I was still elated from the experience and pumped to share it with him. "This is amazing," he said, blown away by the myriad of insights. But then he paused and asked, "So how does this help me?"

His question stopped me in my tracks, pulling me out of the euphoria I was still feeling. And he followed with, "How does this help anyone get rid of their trauma?"

I fell silent for a moment, allowing doubt to pour in. I had expected his reaction to be astonishment, not questions. Both were great inquiries — but I wasn't sure I had the answers. I felt defeated. Since the channeling came through, I was beaming and in awe of all the revelations, and in that next moment, I felt like I was just told: *So what.*

He didn't mean it that way. *But that's how I heard it.*

I felt myself being condensed by fear as concerning questions flooded my mind. *What if this material doesn't change anything? Does this really help anyone? What if no one cares?* And perhaps the most glaring piece that was missing, the channeling was *adamant* about lightening up but never said *how.*

My instinct was to react, defend myself, and defend the information. But instead, I paused. I allowed those thoughts to *move through* without getting stuck in the fear and self doubt. This time, I was more *aware* of my fear and much more aware of how quickly my energy *shifted*.

And if I can shift *into* fear that quickly, I can shift *out* of it just as fast. Our guidance is always whispering to us, but it's difficult to hear through the density. When we lift the fog, inspiration shines through.

That pause after his questions gave me space. The space I needed to allow the fear to pass and allow insight to follow. Barry was actually guiding me to think about next steps. To think about how to harness this experience to bring healing to people. I needed to give myself time to sit with it and feel into the next steps, away from the weight of fear.

Perspective can be a funny thing when we're shrouded in the fog of density. A situation itself just is — not good or bad. It's our own perspective and interpretation of something that causes what we perceive as problems. And it's doubt in our ability to intuitively solve something that feeds our fear.

There's nothing wrong with being afraid. Really, there's nothing *wrong* with anything. And so instead of reacting, instead of defending, I paused to allow room for awareness. To witness my energy condensing. I allowed myself to feel the fear, then chose differently — to allow it to move through and clear the way for inspired thoughts.

Evolution is a process, and each step forward begins with a shift in awareness.

You know that person searching everywhere for their glasses, and they're sitting on top of their head? Whether it dawned on them, or someone else pointed it out, finding the glasses allowed them to stop looking and move forward with clearer vision. They just needed the awareness to realize that what they were searching for was already with them.

Maybe the channeling wasn't supposed to deliver all the answers — because I already had them. It wanted me to look deeper inside myself and into the practices I had been learning, living, and offering for decades. It was the underlying purpose to why I founded AWAKEN Center for Human Evolution. I had been helping people lighten up for the past twelve years!

Once this obvious truth dawned on me, I was reminded that life is always preparing us, giving us exactly what we need, exactly when we need it. I had already built the answers to my own questions. I just needed to *become aware* of it.

Evolution is a process of constant expansion, learning more, understanding more, and always moving forward. That's the mindset we cultivate, immerse ourselves in, and teach at AWAKEN.

I had always spelled AWAKEN in all caps and one day felt guided to give it an acronym. When I sat with it, the words rapidly emerged:

Awareness
Wholeness
Authenticity
Kindness
Empathy
Nurturing

I have a sign with that acronym hanging above my desk to remind me of those words every day. It's amazing how efficiently the universe works behind the corridors of space and time. The answer to the question, *how do we lighten up*, had been there all along: *It begins with awareness.*

This material brings in a new shift in awareness that alters how we perceive life. It shifted mine, and by reading this book, you've now shifted yours, too.

The beauty of awareness is there's no going back. Once the door of awareness opens, you can't close it. I say door, but it's really a portal. A portal opening into a new way of seeing and experiencing life. You can't put the toothpaste back in the tube, and you can't un-know what you're now aware of.

And that's a dangerous thing for us humans, because now we're no longer living in ignorance. We can't hide behind it. We have to *choose* to live in ignorance, ignoring what we know — or live in *awareness.*

When we witness things through the eyes of awareness, we're no longer viewing life as the victim. Being human isn't about surviving our pain. It's about freeing it. We didn't come here to be coddled. *We came here to evolve.* We signed up for the advanced class. We're here to thrive. We were never broken. Only blocked. And I believe our salvation comes from restoring the flow of our energy.

Healing is nothing more, and nothing less, than unblocking the density we've accumulated. We are meant to live with ease, in peace, with the divine creative force of the universe flowing freely through us. When we block that flow, we cut ourselves off from the bliss of creation. What remains, we label as suffering. We give so much power to that word, but suffering is what we feel when we only see an echo of our true self, a shadow of our brilliant light.

Life follows a simple flow: Experience—Choose—Create.

We experience life. We are a witness to it, as well as being a witness to our memory of it. When we live unconsciously, without awareness, we skip the most important step: choice. We move from experience to reaction, bypassing our own free will. And when we live from reaction, we live with a belief that we are helpless victims to life happening around us and ignore our power as creators.

When we witness life with conscious awareness, something shifts. We see the experience for what it is: energy either flowing with life or resisting life.

In that space, we get to choose what comes next. How we respond. What action we take. Or sometimes more importantly, when we pause. What we hold onto and what we allow to pass through. We can then put intention and action into creating the world we want to experience next.

Experience—Choose—Create. Experience what we create. *Infinitely.*

How we live this cycle, with resistance or with flow, is always in our hands. As we lighten up, our experience of creation shifts, allowing us to clearly create what we desire, rather than experience more of what we fear, hate, or resist.

When we understand and embrace who we are and why we are here, we can release suffering and adopt experience. We don't have to like all of our experiences, but we do need to feel them to process them. So feel every moment. Cry. Scream. Hate. Be afraid for as long as it takes — but remember, it's your choice to *stay* in those emotions. You alone hold the power to feel them and *the power to release them.*

As we begin to understand the weight we've been carrying, a new phase begins: shedding what was never ours. The shields we've raised, the walls we've built, the judgements we've carried — all of it was to justify our reactions, none of which reflects our true being. As we release, we reclaim our light.

So many of us question our self worth, never fully realizing the immense role our souls took on. Life is about so much more than just ourselves. It's about our effect on all those we know, on the world around us, and on future generations. Our soul's journey, and this present life, is woven into the larger tapestry of existence.

Even when we deflect what we didn't heal, something inside us knows. There's always some awareness, conscious or not, that when we pass on the pain, we wish we hadn't. In those unseen moments of private repentance, subtle healing occurs. Less and less trauma gets passed on. The lineage lightens, even when no one realizes it's happening.

We're a young species. Still learning. Still finding our footing in the mud. Those of us who understand why we're here see our sacrifices for what they are: taking on dense experiences to have the power to release them. We are the ones who can finally drop the weight. Who can loosen their grip. Who can allow ourselves to lighten up and let the energy move.

So who are you, underneath it all? Under the density, the weight, the inherited patterns, and the survival defenses? Who is that innocent being who first arrived in this world?

You are divine light, a facet of the infinite creative force of the universe, that chose to enter this dense, beautiful, tangled reality with purpose. You arrived expanded. Clear. Fully yourself.

And then life happened.

Layer by layer, experience by experience, the weight accumulated. The barriers went up. You adapted. You survived. But the light of who you are never faded — it was only blocked. You worked with what you were given and what you were taught. And for most of us, that wasn't much when it came to understanding fear and releasing trauma.

That density is not who you are. It's what you became when you stopped experiencing life, blocking it instead of accepting it. You were taught, directly or indirectly, that feeling led to pain. Openness turned to heartbreak. Vulnerability was weakness. The safest thing to do was shut down, hide, and protect yourself. But those responses are not the truth of who you are. They were survival mechanisms. And once we see them for what they are, we can begin to dismantle them.

Simple Truth: You are not your pain, your trauma, or your walls. You are the light behind them.

Fear takes many forms, including mistrust and a persistent sense that we're not enough. We develop a negative relationship with ourselves and the world because of all the unhealed pain being passed on and deflected. We're taught by example to complain about what we don't want, imagine the worst, distrust first, and brace for what might go wrong. We grew up swimming in countless levels of fear, and it's taken a toll on our energy. How can we blame anyone for living in constant fear and anxiety?

We can't.

Except here's where the tables turn — we are the only ones who control *our* fear. Remember, *fear is a choice.*

Even when fear arises as a reaction, the reaction itself lasts only an instant. What follows is still a choice, conscious or unconscious, to hold onto it. Until we make the conscious decision to let it go, we grip it tighter, because that's what we've trained ourselves to do without even realizing it.

When we bring awareness to any situation, it shifts unconscious reactions into conscious decisions. We can choose to see fear as the gift that it is. Fear gives us the opportunity to remember who we are. It's an opportunity to reclaim our power from anyone who stole it — from anyone we gave it to.

Accepting that fear is a choice shifts you into *empowerment*, giving you power over fear. You can *choose to not be afraid.* You can choose joy, faith, and expansion. It doesn't mean the world instantly changes. *It means you do.*

You hold the power to shift your perception, and when you do, your energy instantly shifts. The moment you choose to release fear, your density begins to lighten. And that's when everything begins to change.

It's time to live as an evolved human, living from awareness instead of reaction. From intuition over survival instinct. When we live from conscious choice, meeting life as it comes, feeling what arises, and allowing it to move through rather than building new walls to keep it out, we regain power by lightening up. And the lighter we are, the more fear slips away.

Your light was never gone. It was right behind your walls, waiting to be freed. Waiting to shine as bright as it did when you first arrived. And here is where the illusion breaks down entirely — darkness has no control over us.

Darkness has no power of its own. It has no substance and so it cannot take away our light. It is simply what remains when there is no light. *A shadow isn't created by darkness. It's created by something blocking the light.* And that something is the density we accumulated. Darkness can't take away who we are, but we can relinquish who we are to the fear of darkness.

Even though we've been hiding in our own shadow, the light has never left our side. Never once faltering or flickering. Ever present. Ever radiating. We blocked it out, then blamed the world for having too much darkness.

Shame, anger, hate, emptiness — so much of what we've been calling our darkness is nothing more than the shadow we created within ourselves. Which means we also have the power to dissolve it, allowing shadow to wash away into light.

But we don't tear down the walls by force. Force only thickens them. This isn't about fighting the ego or punishing yourself for how long the walls have stood. It's about seeing a deeper truth: The very pain you've been running from is the doorway back to yourself.

We dissolve the walls through awareness, compassion, and presence. Through the willingness to finally experience what we've been deflecting. When we allow what is no longer needed to crumble, what was always true begins to shine through once again.

Walls block pain, but they also block love and connection. As we begin breaking down the walls, we meet parts of ourselves we've abandoned. This part of the journey may feel scary, vulnerable, even painful. It's also where healing begins.

Be patient with yourself. Sometimes we blast open the gates. Sometimes we only move a pebble. Even if you have to remove one block at a time, it's progress. But honestly, it really is about blasting open the floodgates.

For me, this material sent my walls tumbling down. I wasn't just given a glimpse of truth. I was blown away by it. Because after two decades of spiritual living, I was finally ready to hear it.

And when you're ready, you'll hear it too. No one but you can discover your road to expansion. Sometimes it takes decades, sometimes moments. Whatever your path looks like, know that choosing it is enough to begin. And then all of the universe will step in to help you remember the truth of who you are. The reminders from the universe are always there, and we'll see them when we're ready.

That's why I'm writing this. If you can bring enough awareness to the density you took on, if you can see what your parents couldn't heal, understand it, and understand they did the best they could, then you can be the one to finally free it.

And while fear holds us back in many ways, I ask one thing of you, if nothing else. Never allow fear to prevent you from getting help, whatever form that takes: a therapist, a spiritual guide, a trusted friend, a healing practice, a community. The resources are everywhere. That's why I created AWAKEN. Reach out to me, and if I don't have what you need, I'll point you in the right direction and connect with others who can help. Seek help until you find what's right for you. *You are worth that effort.*

Underneath everything you've carried, everything you've survived, everything that hardened you along the way — it all led to this moment. You came in knowing the cost, *and you came anyway.* The world is sitting in its own shadow, waiting for your light to shine again.

You are still that bright, expansive being of light.

You always were. You always will be.

Now it's time to lighten up, and let it flow.

CHAPTER 11:

Living Lighter

Sometimes I think spirituality ruined my life.

Early on, as my own awakening dawned, a lot about my life changed. Not all at once, but fast enough. I chose to work freelance instead of a full time job, which strained me financially. I stopped drinking and going to bars and clubs every weekend, which distanced me from my long time friends. Every time I dated a new woman, I had to ask myself, *Will this last if she's not interested in spiritual growth?*

Neither my friends nor the women I was meeting were going to sit and meditate with me for an hour or join me for a crystal bowl sound bath. But the area that I struggled with the most was with my family.

As I embraced my spiritual life, the tension created between me and my brother was almost unbearable, and even more so with my father. My dad was strong in his catholic faith and saw this as a betrayal not only to our religion, but in a sense, to him.

In addition, he was recovering from a massive heart attack and there was extra concern about the stress I was "causing" him by veering from "my" religion. But nothing felt right about staying devoted to a religion I didn't choose and didn't always agree with. So I slowly and assuredly chose my own path. The one that was right for me.

Would I have done anything different along the way if I could? *Maybe*. Would I still choose awakening, awareness, and walking a spiritual path? *Every time*.

Living a spiritual life opened doors to amazing new friends and experiences. It was after making the conscious choice to only date conscious minded women that I met my wife. It led me to founding AWAKEN, to channeling this book, and to receiving even more Simple Truths of Existence. Regarding my brother, while he still may not fully understand me and my path, he fully supports me. He's been a core member of the AWAKEN board from its inception, and for that I am grateful.

This channeling shifted my awareness to a new level. But awareness alone isn't the whole journey. It's just the beginning — *an essential, beautiful beginning*. Knowing why we carry the weight doesn't automatically lift it. Understanding the mechanics of our density doesn't instantly dissolve it. Insight opens the door. And now we have to walk through it. This material creates a path to a new way of *perceiving* life. And now we have to be brave enough to alter how we react to life and how we *live it*.

Simple Truth: When we live through awareness, we stop responding through reaction.

Lightening up isn't a metaphor. It's a reality played out at the level of our energy, our particles, and the very essence of our being.

When we condense our energy through fear, trauma, walls, and resistance, we become like a rock. Dense. Rigid. Impenetrable. When energy comes our way in this state, it can't pass through. It hits us and stops. That's not a flaw. That's not weakness. That's physics. Two rocks colliding can't pass through each other. When our beliefs clash, the energy has nowhere to go.

But when we lighten up, something extraordinary happens. We expand. We give our energy space. We open up at the particle level, the way gas particles space out. We begin allowing everything to move through us freely, and we freely move through life. In that expanded state, energy doesn't hit us — it passes through. We experience it. We feel it. We're even changed by it, but we don't hold onto it. We don't get weighed down by it. And we don't have to pass it on.

That's the simple truth of it all, that three hours of teachings boiled down to: *all we had to do was allow the energy to pass through*. The mistake was thinking we either had to hold it in or keep it out. We were never supposed to stop it. The real choice, that changes everything, is choosing to let it pass through.

But this is about more than lightening up dense energy. It's about lightening up our minds, our beliefs, and our attachments. Lightening up means not getting stuck in old ways of thinking. Not gripping tightly to how things used to be or how we think they should be. Not allowing attachment to anchor us to the past when creation is always moving forward. The wave of creation never stops. The only question is whether we're moving with it, enjoying the ride, or fighting the current, struggling to not drown. If you feel like you're tumbling into the undertow of life, out of control and powerless against it — it may be time to lighten up and get back into the flow.

As we lighten up allowing energy to pass through us, something equally beautiful happens: we allow more light to pass through. Denser matter blocks light — that's why caves are dark. Expansive energy allows space for light, so the more expansive we are, the more light shines through. As we lighten up, we allow more light in and also allow more light to radiate out. As we expand, we quite literally en-lighten ourselves and the world.

We are the sovereign rulers of our own energy. The choice is now ours to hold onto our density, or live a lighter life. There was a moment during the channeling that really drove this home. I had a vision of particles interacting with each other in a fun and playful way, a beautiful reflection of what the states of matter teach us. I saw a gas particle embodying the energy of a hippie — free, loving, and light:

A gas is floating along and meets a large solid object. The gas can't pass through the solid because it's too dense. The gas stops, and the gas particle says, "Hey man, I can't pass through unless you lighten up."

The solid refuses to change. It keeps its particles packed tightly together, armored up, shields ready for impact. The solid particles call out, "Stay together. Stand your ground. Don't let anything through!"

And the gaseous hippie particle, accepting of all things, says, "Right on. If you want to stay solid, if you want to be dense, that's cool. I came here to experience you, to experience everything, man. But I'm not here to judge. If you want to keep to yourself and not experience me, it's groovy. I'll just flow around you." And the gas goes on its way.

Next, the gas meets another gas, and they pass right through each other with ease. Their particles wave as they pass each other by, saying, "Far out, man. Good to see you. Come on through."

They fully experience each other, entangling and connecting. "Right on. High five on the way out. See you next time around. Peace out." The particles give each other high fives and float off into other experiences, entangled on a quantum level and connected throughout time and space.

The gas continues floating along, and sees a dense mass labeled as evil heading its way. The gas had encountered evil before, and had nothing to fear. Feeling the low vibes of evil but understanding and loving all things, the hippie particle says, "Oh, hey evil. Thanks for being here, man. Thanks for being part of creation. I'm just gonna expand myself and let you pass on through." And both the hippie particles and the evil particles continue on their journeys.

When we meet a dense, resistant energy — like what we might call evil — we can be the rock, standing our ground and ready to clash, or we can be like the gas, allowing it to move through us so we can effortlessly continue our journey of life.

And here's what's so liberating about this: It shows us that we don't need anyone else to change but ourselves. When two people are arguing, fighting, holding firmly to their beliefs — it's a stalemate. Like two rocks banging into each other, neither getting anywhere. But it only takes one of them to lighten up. The moment we expand our energy and stop resisting, the other person can remain as dense as they want, and they no longer affect us. Their density passes through like a block of ice falling through water. No clash. No collision. No pain passed on. We don't need the whole world to lighten up to live in peace. We only need to lighten up ourselves.

Life is full of encounters like these. The more impactful the experience, the deeper it's imprinted in our energy.

When we travel to other countries, they stamp our passport. The stamp doesn't mean the country controls us, or that we have to stay there. It doesn't mean we only speak that language even after we leave. It means: *I've been there. I experienced it. I know more about it.* The architecture, the food, the culture — we're now entangled with it. We brought home knowledge and experience of that place. It's something to be proud of, and how it affects us is our choice.

Maybe it brings us a new appreciation for its people, and we find ourselves connecting more warmly when we cross paths with someone from that country. Maybe we seek out more authentic food because it brings back happy memories. Or maybe we had an experience we never want to repeat, and choose never to return — but that choice is ours to make, now grounded in our own personal experience.

That's what our most difficult experiences are. That's what evil is. Stamps on our passport. *I've been there. I've experienced it.* And now we can choose to let go of resistance without choosing to feed the energy of evil, and go on with creation.

Every hardship, every heartbreak, every wall we built — those are stamps in a passport that proves we showed up. That we were brave enough, or simply open enough, to fully engage with this wild, dense, complicated existence rather than ignore it, fight it, or keep our distance from it.

Own your passport. Every stamp in it. Not because the hard trips traumatized you, but because they made you the seasoned soul traveler of life that you are — experienced, expanded, and ready for the next journey.

And remember, the traveler is not the place they visited. You are not your pain. You are not your trauma. You are the one who went there, experienced it, and now it's time to return home, altered, and if you choose — expanded.

That's lightness. That's letting the experience of creation pass through. That's the whole point. Evolution is about evolving to higher states. We're not meant to live as rocks. Not even water.

A i r .

Expansive. Open. Light enough to let life pass through us instead of resisting it, instead of colliding with it.

Think about how big the universe is for a moment: vast, open, and more immense than we can fathom. The natural state of existence is expansion. As humans, it's our nature to reproduce, explore, and experience new things. From traveling to other countries and experiencing new cultures, creating and eating new foods, to developing and incorporating amazing new technology — expansion is our natural state of being.

Next time the density is weighing down, remember to live like hippie particles — free and light. And to help you along the way, I'd like to share my experience of what living lighter looks like in everyday life.

Learning to live lighter starts with awareness, and as we integrate new lessons and insights into our being, we apply them and begin living them. Lightening up is not always a dramatic shift overnight — not a lightning bolt moment or a three-hour channeling. Expanding your awareness comes in waves, often in unexpected moments. The big shifts in our energy and how we live are more about the quiet, consistent practice of *noticing, understanding, and choosing differently.* As we make little shifts in our daily routines, we see big shifts in our life.

Become more aware of your energy. Notice when it condenses. Notice when fear creeps in, even if it's under the guise of logic or protection. Notice when you're reacting instead of consciously choosing. Ask yourself: *What am I afraid of?* And then ask: *What if I choose to release this fear?*

When you feel yourself contracting, tightening, shutting down, and becoming defensive, that's your signal. Not that the enemy is approaching, but that your walls are still up, still trying to block some part of creation. That's your invitation to deliberately and consistently let go of blocks and ask: *What am I resisting?*

Being more in tune with your own energy creates the space for making new choices. This is where patterns become visible. The ones we never questioned because we inherited them: addictions, compulsive thoughts, and stuck ways of doing things that keep recycling the same energy. These aren't flaws. They're stuck energy looking for a way out. When you see them for what they are, you stop fighting them and start asking: *What is this trying to release?*

Notice others' reactions, too. Especially the reactions of those closest to you. When you remember it's their pain calling out for help and not a personal attack, your perception shifts. And that shift puts you in a place of *responding* instead of *reacting*. If you can stand in the gravitational pull of someone else's trauma and respond with love, you shine light directly into their black hole. You remind them that it's not who they are, and that they, too, have a choice.

Living lighter extends into every interaction — how we speak to our coworkers, our friends, our family. Especially our children. The souls of our children didn't come here to be managed or controlled. They came here to help shift us, to help recreate the world. Every time a child triggers a reaction, that's not a parenting failure — that's an opportunity to apply everything we now know. To pause instead of react. To choose awareness over defense.

One of the most important concepts that this wisdom has instilled in me is that *it's always about the energy*. Everything we say, think, and do is a byproduct of the underlying energy. Shift the energy, and it instantly shifts our response. The energy drives the reaction, and our response reflects the level of our consciousness, coming either from a place of pain or a place of light.

Every confrontation, every harsh word, every issue someone has with someone else — it's never about the words. It's about the unhealed pain looking for somewhere to go. When someone comes at us with anger, criticism, or cruelty, we're feeling their trapped energy pressing against us. And we have two choices.

We can receive it with compassion, understanding the pain beneath it. Or we can react — because their pain resonated with ours, pressing on a tender spot we haven't yet healed. When we view every interaction as energy responding to energy, we disarm any personal feelings and are aware enough to respond differently.

There are so many opportunities in our lives to lighten up. Become the witness to every one of them. See them as ways to expand, instead of contract. As we own our energy, we can redirect it in positive directions. Every choice we make ripples outward. Once we know how to lighten up, we can go beyond understanding it and live it.

When you feel yourself resisting something, whether it's a person, an idea, or the thought of doing something, pause. Take a moment to feel the density around the resistance. Feel into why you might be resisting this. And go deeper than the surface thoughts, thoughts like I don't like this person, or I don't like doing this. It's okay to not *resonate* with something. The question is *why are you reacting to it?* That's where you need to lighten up.

This journey isn't about perfection or self-judgement. It's about getting to know yourself from an energetic perspective — witnessing your patterns, your reactions, your fears, and your light with equal curiosity and compassion. The more honestly we see ourselves, the more naturally we begin to shift. And as we lighten up and shift our frequencies, things we no longer resonate with begin to drift away on their own.

Support your energy by doing things that help you feel lighter. Find ways to give. Go out of your way to help others. Volunteer. Donate. Give back in whatever way calls to you. These are the types of actions that expand us, that lighten us up.

Laugh more. Play more. Spend time in nature — barefoot. Ground into the Earth's natural frequency. Try meditation, breathwork, sound healing, and yoga. Not because you should, but because they work. They move energy. They crack open the door.

The energy you immerse yourself in is the level of energy you resonate with. This isn't a judgement. It's physics. Ask yourself: *Do the things I bring into my life, body, and awareness feed fear and drama or feed expansion?* Pay attention to what you eat, watch, listen to, and who you spend time with. They all directly affect your frequency and ability to hold a lighter state of being. Your body and your energy field will tell you what raises your vibration and what lowers it. Listen to both.

Find what is calling you: a practice, teacher, book, or event. That pull is your soul pointing toward the next step. Honor it. One step leads to the next. The universe will guide you from there. And you'll also feel when it's time to move on to something different. A new teacher or community. The journey of evolution and lightening up is always in motion.

We create a very different and beautiful energy collectively. If you don't have conscious minded people in your life, look for some. Make new personal connections and seek out conscious communities online and in person. There are more of us than you realize.

Gravitate towards people who understand the language of energy. Who understand what it looks like when the walls come down. We need mirrors. We need people who remind us of who we really are when the density gets thick.

And remember, you are consciousness first. You don't have to go anywhere to shift your energy. Visualization is a powerful tool. On an energetic level, it can be as real as any experience. Imagination and memory stir emotions. Use them to draw in energy that fills you with lightness.

Sometimes it feels like we're addicted to our wounds. And in a way, we are. Not because we want the pain, but because we've been vibrating at that frequency for so long, we've become used to it. We've attuned ourselves to the frequency of our trauma. It takes a little extra energy to pull ourselves out of a familiar vibration, even when that vibration is hurting us.

It's okay to be afraid and push yourself out of your comfort zone. Feel it. Allow it, and do it anyway. Allow space for the universe to surprise you. You may surprise yourself along the way.

Every new door you open expands you in new directions. And when you find an unexpected new door and you feel that fear creeping in, pause. Take a moment, take a breath, ask for guidance, and trust the answer is on its way.

Simple Truth: Lightening up allows space for the energy of creation to flow through.

If I've learned nothing else from the Simple Truths material, it's that the answers to life are always right in front of us, and so much more obvious than we realize.

Perhaps the biggest challenge for us to overcome is that the answers to life are simple — so simple, we don't want to believe it.

We're in disbelief over how complicated our minds can make things. How strongly density traps us. How tightly the gravity of our trauma holds us. Because believing the answer to all our pain could be simple means accepting something uncomfortable: that the choice has always been ours. That our energy was never controlled by forces outside of us. And that regardless of what we experienced, holding onto fear, trauma, and victimhood has been our own decision.

And that's a hard truth to sit with. Because so many of us have spent years, even decades, dedicated to our pain. Defining ourselves by it. Building our identity around it. If we release it, who are we? What does life mean without it? And perhaps the hardest realization and question to ask: Why would I have held onto all this pain if it were up to me to let it go?

This is the final wall. And it's the most important one to bring down. Because we can't play victim anymore. It means we are responsible for our own happiness — for our own light, or lack of it. What if life really is simple? What if all we need to do to live happy and free is choose to? What if we are the only ones holding ourselves prisoner to fear?

When I first heard *just release it* as the answer to releasing fear, my reaction was disbelief. But what if the answer *is* that simple? What if releasing all our pain, trauma, and suffering is a choice? A choice that requires us to let go. To trust not only in life, but in ourselves — and each other. Trust that we collectively have the power to change the world, remembering that each individual also has the power to change the collective.

But no matter how many signs the universe sends us, and no matter how obvious the truth may really be, our density fogs our lenses and distorts our view of reality. So as we embark on this journey of lightening up, I offer one last piece of insight: *Be gentle with yourself.*

This magnificent life is yours, and it's unfolding exactly as it should. Learning to lighten up is easy, but it may feel hard — that's your density holding on. Shifting generational trauma takes time. Our lineage has been passing on their density for lifetimes. But each generation has also been slowly releasing it.

Genealogy holds powerful energy. Our genes are conscious, carrying a record of every generation that came before us. They remember the pain, yes, but also the love, the sacrifice, and the quiet moments of healing that happened in the dark. And here is the breathtaking truth: When we release that generational pain, we don't just free ourselves. We change the story encoded in our very cells. We create a new energy, a new possibility — not just for ourselves, but for every soul who comes after us.

All things happen in the time they need, especially growth. It may take generations, or decades, or you might be completely transformed in a year. Our struggles also create our strength. Free a butterfly too soon, and its wings aren't strong enough to fly. A butterfly knows that it's ready to emerge when it has the strength to break down the walls surrounding it. If it's strong enough to break through its cocoon, it has the ability to fly, gliding effortlessly through the air.

It takes energy to pull us up and out of the vibration we've been living in. That accumulated energy is strong. The pressure of density, drama, and trauma is all around us. Even as we choose to lift ourselves out of it, it will occasionally pull us back in. And that's okay. We also need to lighten up about lightening up, or we'll end up adding more density to our energy instead of releasing it. We are humans, waking up in the middle of a dense and complicated existence and choosing, again and again, to expand.

As your own density lifts, you'll naturally want to help others lift theirs, and remind them who they are. Offer advice, insight, and experience, all while allowing each individual's journey to unfold as it will. We're here to change creation, but not by uncreating. So don't assume it's your job to force anyone else to do things differently. The fastest way for us all to evolve isn't by telling others how they should live, but by living our own lives lighter.

By offering more light to the world, we stop passing on pain, unblock the density, and break down the walls of defense.

Our free will is the greatest superpower we'll ever have. If we wish to see a more enlightened world, we need to shine more light into it. Put more intention and desire into seeing ourselves, and all of humanity, grow and evolve. And choose, every day, things that lighten us up.

If each of us continues to choose lighter ways of thinking, doing, and being, I promise you, it will become our new standard. Our new frequency.

Others will feel it. Resonate with it. And they, too, will want to live lighter and be free.

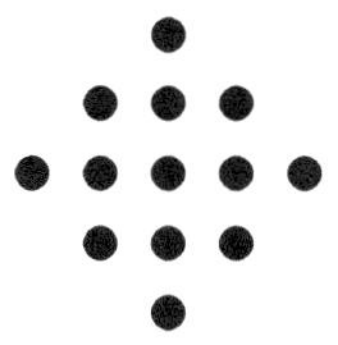

Expanding Onward

The book ends here. The journey doesn't.

I walk through this life with immense reverence for every soul, and I commend those who chose the big roles in this theater of life. The ones who chose to move the energy for not only themselves, but for the collective. For every person who carried more than their share so that the energy could move. If you don't yet realize the immense importance of your life, the role you play, the density you release, the light you carry, I hope this book changes that. Even if just a little.

We've only just scratched the surface of this reality. This wisdom, this book, and the others in this series, are just a small piece of this vast, unfolding puzzle of our existence.

The full meaning of life is an immense mystery — far grander than our condensed minds can fully grasp right now. But as we expand, we expand into that grander truth of why we are here. What became clear through this material is that the truth of life is also far simpler than we've imagined.

Life was designed to make our lessons obvious, our path visible, and the way forward as clear as possible. We have legions of loving beings by our side every moment waiting to offer guidance. And all of creation reflects and responds to our current energy — so we can always see where we are, how we got here, and where we're headed.

The question that echoed in my mind, I now offer to you: *Now what?*

Now it becomes *your choice*.

You are already more aware than you were yesterday. Now it's up to you to choose if you want to keep expanding.

Awakening isn't dramatic moments of transformation. It's a thousand small choices, made daily. Choosing expansion over contraction. Awareness over reaction. Flow over resistance.

It's in making these choices, moment by moment, that we return to the innocent, childlike place we began — where lightness is our natural way of being.

You Are Never Alone

Humanity has an infinite amount of support surrounding us. Every one of us — here and now — has legions of beings on the other side who are always with us. They exist outside of the confines of space and time. Our entire lifetime is simply a moment for them.

They have never left your side. Not in your darkest moment. Not when you felt most alone. Not when the density was so thick you couldn't feel anything beyond it. They were there with you.

They still are. They're waiting, with total devotion, for you to open up enough to receive the love and guidance they've been pouring in all along.

Call on them — your guides, angels, ancestors, source, the universe, even God. They hear you every time. Every prayer is received and answered. If you haven't felt or heard the response, it's not because it wasn't sent — it's because the density that surrounds you interferes with the signal. That's the cruel irony of it. Our own dense walls have the power to deafen us from the voices of all those trying to reach us. But as the walls come down, as the energy starts to move, the channel opens.

That is why those struggling the most, in the darkest and densest moments of their life, will hit their lowest point before seeing the light — because it is in that moment of giving up that we give in. We release. We no longer have the energy to keep up our walls and hold our blocks in place, and in that most desperate moment, the door cracks open, letting in just enough light to facilitate change. And sometimes we let go so completely, we instantly lighten up. That's the beauty and power of surrender.

You were never meant to do this alone. And you never have. I promise you.

Already There

I know where humanity is going. I have imagined it, seen it, and felt it in the deepest moments of this work. I know it is possible in our lifetime — if enough of us make the choice. By reading this book, you've already begun.

There is a version of us that is already healed. Already unified. Already living in flow and in peace.

I can see it clearly. Healed parents raising children who remain in the light, growing up in tune with themselves, others, and all of life — including the Earth herself. Children who are free to experience life for themselves. To choose what they love and what they don't. To learn in the ways that call to them. To live how they want, love who they want, stay true to who they are.

Imagine a child running toward the street, chasing a ball, fully present and aware of every step — sensing the traffic, knowing in their body whether it's safe to cross. No parent chasing after them in fear, screaming. No trauma is transferred in that moment because the child's own awareness can be trusted completely. Because awareness was passed on instead of pain.

I see a world where we can disagree and every disagreement comes with genuine understanding of the other perspective. Where companies put humanity first. Where the energy of war has nowhere to take hold because there is no density left to grip. Where the Earth's resources are honored and shared, not owned and withheld.

Sound too far-fetched? I promise you it's not. We just have to embody that level of awareness in ourselves first, and we're already on our way — you, me, and countless others expanding their awareness and energy every day.

There's a world where we live in full expression of what we actually are — creators of reality. It exists. And the only thing standing between that reality and this one is time.

The amount of time it takes *is up to us.*

If each of us makes the choice to live a little more consciously today than yesterday — to stop passing on the pain, to reclaim our true selves, and to lighten up — that timeline collapses. What might have taken a thousand years becomes possible in a generation. Maybe even *this* generation.

So ask yourself: Do you want to live in a world where every child is taught to be afraid — or taught to be aware?

It's not me being overly optimistic or hopeful. It's not naive. It's energy. One person lightening up creates space for the next. A ripple becomes a wave. A wave becomes a shift. A shift creates a new world.

Healing is a return to the natural flow. And the natural flow of this universe — of creation itself — is always toward expansion. Toward love. Toward light.

Simple Truth: To see less darkness in the world, shine more light into it.

Your soul chose to be here, now, to be part of expansion. Not as a victim. Not as a bystander. As a conscious energetic force to shift creation towards something truer. Something brighter. Something lighter.

Go live fully and boldly. Celebrate every stamp in your passport. Every storm that cleared the way. Let it go, lighten up, and allow creation to keep passing through.

The only thing between your density and your freedom is a matter of choice.

And the time to choose is now.

A Gift

Thank you again for being here, for doing this work, and for being brave enough to choose awareness when ignorance often feels easier.

To help you along your journey to lightness, I'd like to offer you a gift — *a workbook*. It's carefully designed to take everything you've explored here, dive deeper into truth, and bring it into your daily life.

This is where we put words into practice and practice into motion. The workbook asks us to be brave enough to look deeper at ourselves, where we've been hurt, and where we've hurt others. Its exercises and visualizations are crafted to help rewire our consciousness and change the way we think, feel, and react.

The workbook includes journaling prompts, self-inquiry, visualization practices, and other tools designed to help you integrate this material — not just as knowledge but as lived experience, because awareness without practice stays in your mind. This wisdom is meant to fill your entire being: mind, body, and spirit.

Download it free at **GregCampisi.com/LightenUp**

We're all here to remind ourselves — and each other — to *lighten up!*

More About the Author and AWAKEN

With immense gratitude, I thank you for reading this book.

I'm Greg Campisi, founder and director of AWAKEN Center for Human Evolution, speaker, author, and channeler. For over three decades, I built my career as a website and graphic designer. As the Simple Truths material began pouring through, something shifted. The guidance became clear. It was time to let go of my identity as a designer and step fully into the role of messenger, teacher, and guide — as an Awakener.

This is my soul's mission. It's why I'm here — to bring this wisdom of the Simple Truths of Existence to every soul ready to receive it through various media and events.

I am here to walk alongside you during your process of awakening, helping you find your own truth, in your own time, in your own way.

I've learned that the path to enlightenment doesn't take perfection, but it takes dedication. You'll know when you're ready. And when you are, I can help open the doors, but only you can walk through them — not as my follower, but as my fellow human being, my companion soul.

After decades of meditating, breathwork, channeling, and building AWAKEN, I still have days when density wins. I am still doing the work, getting triggered, and hitting walls that I've held onto since childhood. But the difference is that I recognize my blocks quicker and dismantle my walls easier. I now understand it all from a new perspective, on a much deeper level.

I know my trauma and my walls are not who I am. I know I'm not broken and there is nothing to fix. I know I am worthy of healing, worthy of love, and worthy of this miraculous life. And so are you.

We all are.

No matter how much density we collected along the way, we're all here to help each other out of it.

I'm here for you — to inspire, to guide, and to awaken you to who you've always known yourself to be.

If you're feeling ready for a deep dive into this life journey, I work with people one on one. These personal sessions are designed to awaken you to the truth of who you are and why you're living this life, here and now.

Whether you're just beginning to wake up or have been on this path for years, these sessions are a space to go deeper, get clearer, and find your next step. You can learn more about my offerings at **GregCampisi.com**.

And AWAKEN's here for you, too. Long before this channeling came through, I heeded the call to create a safe, loving space where people can connect, grow, heal, and expand together.

AWAKEN Center for Human Evolution offers events, expos, community, experiences, and ongoing support for your journey. While nothing replaces the collective energy of gathering in person, the beauty of this moment is that we can connect, learn, and grow with souls all over the world. AWAKEN's online community makes that possible, as well.

Learn more about AWAKEN Center for Human Evolution and its offerings at **AwakenCHE.org**

I offer these options humbly. There are countless other amazingly gifted people and growing communities out there. Find the ones that resonate with you. And what resonates today may shift for you tomorrow. Honor each calling that you have. Each feeling. Each step. And trust in the universe to continually guide you.

Thank you for honoring the brilliant light you are and sharing this journey of creation.

With love, reverence, and full belief in who you are,

Greg Campisi

Founder, AWAKEN Center for Human Evolution

GregCampisi.com | AwakenCHE.org

www.ingramcontent.com/pod-product-compliance
Lightning Source LLC
LaVergne TN
LVHW020047110826
845155LV00029B/665

9798996281909